HOLBROOK

The Story of a Village 1900-1983

THE AUTHOR

Warrenton Page

HOLBROOK

The Story of a Village 1900-1983

WARRENTON PAGE

The Pentland Press
Edinburgh

First published in 1983 by
The Pentland Press
Edinburgh

ISBN 0 946270 03 1

Printed and bound by D. & J. Croal Ltd., Haddington, Scotland
Artist Ann Ross Paterson

To my CHILDREN

GRANDCHILDREN

and GREAT GRANDCHILDREN

especially JAMES — the latest addition.

PREFACE

The author, a splendidly alert octogenarian, relates the story of a Suffolk village during the first half of the Twentieth century. These personal reminiscences, related in a crisp and beautifully modulated prose, which belies the elementary education of its author, constitute an important social document which covers the Great War, the Depression and World War II. Farming methods, employment problems, education, home life and living conditions are all described against the background of hardship and deprivation which covered most of the country between 1900 and 1950: but this is by no means a horror story. Illuminating the anecdotes and descriptions of country life is the ready wit and impish humour of a man whose experiences span the period between the discovery of the South Pole and the invention of the silicon chip. However much we bemoan our contemporary problems, it is perhaps good for us to recall how the problems of an earlier age were faced and overcome.

Iain Mathieson.

Chapter 1
BEGINNINGS

It would probably be of interest to the reader if I told of my family's connection with the Village before the beginning of the Century. My maternal grandfather was Archibald Smith, the eldest son of a family of six, whose mother had come into the locality from Tinmouth in about the year 1835, as a children's nurse. When Archibald was about 13 years old his father died, leaving his mother to bring up this rather large family, which evidently she did, bravely and fairly successfully. Four of this family, three sons and one daughter, remained in the village all their lives and were buried in the churchyard.

My grandfather became the licensee of the 'Compasses Inn' in about the year 1879 and, with the help of his wife and some members of their family, carried on the business, which included selling coal and pork etc. until 1888. He had suffered from a spinal complaint for rather a long time and during the last two or three years of his life was confined to his bed. When he died at the comparatively early age of 51 years, my grandmother was granted the licence, and carried on until 1899.

The Compasses Inn. 1907.

Our Family Homes 1900-1909.
(Burnt down 1919).

My mother, who was the youngest of a family of six, married my father (Harry Page) in 1896. They lived with, and assisted my grandmother with the business until her death. I think my grandmother must have been a very brave and capable woman, because as well as losing her husband she lost a son aged 23 years and a daughter aged 22 years, all three deaths occurring within six years.

In the early part of 1900 my parents moved into rooms at Brown's Farm, and in June of the same year I was born — so I really did begin life at the beginning of the Century. In 1901 my father was able to hire a small thatched cottage, one of three, which stood where the present petrol filling station is now situated. At that time the village was quite small and compact and it was an interesting spot to live, as most of the inhabitants would pass by at least once a week. As a result, I had learned a lot about the habits and activities of the local people by the time I had reached the age of 5 years, and from what my parents told me I think it would be true to say that I knew Holbrook as it had been at the beginning of the Century.

There were at that time two distinct types of village, known as 'Open' and 'Closed', the latter being those in which the Squire owned most, if not all, of the land and property, and therefore employed the majority of workers. Holbrook would have been classified as an Open Village, with three owners of land, namely the Berners family at Woolverstone Hall, the Rodwell family at The Woodlands, and a

Mr G. Reade at Holbrook House. There were also several owners of small blocks of dwelling houses. This explains why life in Holbrook was so very different to that in nearby Woolverstone, for instance, where Squire Berners owned and controlled everything, including sporting events. The noticeable differences between Holbrook and Woolverstone were that in Holbrook the workers had a choice of employment, there was a possibility of hiring a cottage that was not classed as a tied cottage, and there was an opportunity for more people to have a say in the affairs of the village, particularly through the Parish Council.

Before the outbreak of World War One, Holbrook was the natural centre of about half the villages in the Samford Hundred, and the police constables in the area were under the supervision of the sergeant who was stationed there. At this particular time most of the men and lads worked in the village, walking to and from work, as only a few of them had cycles, of which they took great care, using them only in the evenings and on Sundays.

As the farmers were the main employers of labour I will give a few details of each farm:—

The Woodlands Farm was let to Mr Charles Smith, also known as 'Swanky'. He employed three men and a lad, and kept five horses as well as six cows, several head of cattle, and a few pigs and hens. Next to him at the Red House Farm was Mr Henry Cousins, who also employed the same number of workers, and kept about the same number of cattle, etc. Brown's Farm on the same Estate was let to one of my uncles, Mr Tommy Smith. This was called a 'Two Horse Farm', with about 30 acres of land which could not support a worker. In fact, my uncle had to undertake contract work in order to get a living. Brook Farm on the Holbrook House Estate was farmed by another of my uncles, Mr Fred Smith. Once again there was a mixture of live stock and four men. Wall Farm was let to Mr William Fisk, who had been in the village for a short time. This farm was about the same size as Brook Farm, but was more difficult to work as some of the fields were hilly and had seams of strong clay in them. Here six men were employed and the same number of horses were kept. At Alton Green Farm Mr John Lait was the tenant, and he was assisted by his brother, Thomas, and four other men. There were also two sets of farm premises on the Holbrook House Estate, namely, Mark Wells and the New Buildings now occupied by the Works Department of the Royal Hospital School. The land attached to these two farms was worked as one unit by Mr Walter Wrinch of Erwarton Ness. Eleven men worked here, six of whom lived in the Parish. There were four farms that were situated on the parish boundary, namely, Alton Hall, Potassh, Freston Grove, and Red House on the Woolverstone Estate. Twenty-four of the workers on these farms lived in Holbrook, making the total of farm workers about 50 men and 8 boys, as well as 6 maids who worked in the farm houses. The reader may well ask why there were two 'Red House Farms' in one village. I am afraid I cannot give the answer. The locals solved the problem by calling them by the name of the farmer, E. G. Lewin and Cousins.

Most of the farmers kept a few cows, and sold the milk at the back door of the house at specified times — 7.45 a.m. and 4.15 p.m. Boys and girls had to fetch this in cans before and after school, and woe betide anyone who was more than five minutes late. The milk had been skimmed once, and sometimes twice, before it was sold, the price being two pints for one penny, although Mr Cordle at Potassh Farm sold separated milk at three pints for one penny. Only the gentry had new milk and sometimes mothers with new born babies, that is if they were fortunate enough to be given a free ticket for fourteen days' supply of one pint per day. In winter it was quite common for boys to be seen struggling along with only their toes in their boots, their feet swollen with chilblains as a result of getting wet feet.

Chapter 2

BUSINESSMEN IN THE VILLAGE

There were several small businessmen in the village, and they employed over 50 men and several young women as maids, as well as creating work indirectly for many more. As I give the details of self-employed people and small businessmen, you may think that my memory is playing tricks, but I can assure you that there are still other people alive who can verify my recollections.

Butchers — Mr Freeman Allen ran a very successful family butchers business at Reed House (now Reed Hall). He employed 3 men and 2 boys and kept 4 ponies and delivered meat into at least 8 villages. Mr Henry Simson had a small hut on what is now the village hall grounds, and used a barn at Alton Hall for a slaughterhouse. He also delivered meat to the neighbouring villages. Mr William Collinson had a small pork butchers shop at the back of the Swan Inn. All three butchers killed the animals on their premises.

Builders — The family of Mr Walter Wagstaff ran a general building business in the yard of the Sorrel Horse, and employed on average 8 men and kept 3 ponies. Mr C. Munnings had workshops etc. at Green Bank and, as well as contracting for house building, specialized in plumbing, and had 6-8 men on his payroll. He kept one horse for transport. Mr W. Phillips was a self-employed painter.

Brickworks — The brickyard at Holbrook Creek was run by Mr Frank Reade, a brother of the owner of the Estate. Here the number of workers fluctuated between 10 and 30 men. Two horses were kept for moving sand and clay.

Blacksmith — Mr William Stannard was the owner of the forge, and had two assistants. These premises were attached to Jubilee House, and have since been converted into a bungalow.

Wheelwright — Mr Henry Rogers, who had a workshop on an adjoining plot, was the village carpenter, wheelwright, and undertaker, and was also the Church Clerk. He had one man to help him.

Doctors — There were two doctors in the village with separate practices. Dr Mahon had a surgery at Denmark House, and visited patients in every village east of the Ipswich to London Railway Line. He employed a groom, a gardener, and two domestic maids. Later the groom became chauffeur as Dr Mahon was the first person in the village to own a car, a 'De Dion', which had two seats and a 'dicky seat'. This was in 1907. Dr 'Tim' Carey lived at the Beeches, and he too travelled all round the peninsula by pony trap. His hobby was riding and hunting and he kept two hunters, as well as two ponies for the dog car. He employed two men and domestic maids. The grooms employed by both doctors had to sleep on the premises, in readiness for any emergency call, which were fairly frequent as a doctor had to attend every confinement case. There were two separate practices because of the excessive drinking habits of a former doctor, by the name of Fleming, who lived at Denmark House! He had taken the practice from his father who had lived at the Cedars. Dr Fleming, Jnr. found it difficult to keep an assistant, because of his unreasonable behaviour. When Dr Carey disagreed with his boss he did not move to another area as other students had done, but stayed in the village and began another practice, in about the year 1890. He hired two rooms in a house in the Street. Later he moved into the Beeches, and in about 1906 had the detached wooden building erected which served as a surgery, until the present building was erected. In about 1907 Dr Mahon left the village and his practice was taken over by Dr H. P. Sleigh, and after him in 1930 a Dr Scott came to Holbrook. He in turn sold the practice to Dr A. H. Andrews, who at this time lived and practised at the Beeches. So the two practices became one, with Dr P. L. Crosbie as the partner.

Dairy — Miss Sophia Rodwell of the Woodlands kept a small herd of Jersey cows at Hither House, and sold the milk and butter locally, using what is now the butchers shop as a dairy. A Mr Overall was cowman, and his wife looked after the dairy. In about 1907 Miss Rodwell moved the cows to some sheds in the Halesgrove area, and had a dairy built in the garden of one of the thatched cottages which stood nearby. These cottages were demolished only a few years ago. The premises at Hither House were taken over by Mr H. Simson, who had previously had a small butchers hut in the Street.

Carriers — There were two carriers who travelled to Ipswich every day of the week, except Sundays and Wednesdays. Mr William Stiff had a four-wheeled van, which was drawn by two black mares. These were well fed and groomed, and were stabled in some sheds at the back of the blacksmith's shop, until about 1907. Many of the villagers were unable to go into Ipswich very often and so made use of Bill Stiff, better known as 'Dilla', to do their shopping. He did this very efficiently — even to buying corsets etc! If a woman did decide to go and do her shopping it meant a long day out. 'Dilla's' bugle would sound about 9 a.m., and when the passengers had all been seated the six mile journey began. As there would be several stops on the way, it would be nearly eleven o'clock when they arrived at the Waggon & Horses in the Buttermarket. The return journey began at about 3.30 p.m. and ended one and a half hours later, at the Post Office. Dilla had to go through the village delivering the parcels he had collected in town. The other carrier, Mr Percy Abbott, lived at Lower Holbrook in a thatched house that stood where Brook House is now situated. He drove a one-horse-van, and left Holbrook Post Office at about 11 a.m., which was very convenient for anyone wishing to go into Ipswich for a shorter period. Both men had regular customers, including the small shopkeepers who would travel in the van and go to the wholesalers themselves, but as one man said — "If I'm in a hurry I walk!"

Market Gardeners — Mr William Catchpole lived at the Hermitage and cultivated a few acres that surrounded the buildings. He kept two horses, and on Saturday mornings would load his van with fruit and vegetables and travel into Ipswich to sell his produce — mostly to householders in the Wherstead Road area. He was also a coal and wood merchant, and had quite a thriving business. In the winter months he employed two men in the woods at Freston, cutting and tying faggot wood which he retailed around the villages nearby for kindlingwood, and brick oven firing. Mr James Ling lived in some thatched cottages at the back of The Sorrel Horse. He grew quite a lot of produce on the church allotments and also purchased some from cottagers, and took them into Ipswich on Wednesdays and Saturdays. Sometimes he would bring back a box of bloaters or other fish and sell them in the village. A son of James Ling, known as 'Little Billie' because he was deformed, owned a pony and a 'waggonette' (a four wheeled vehicle) in which he used to convey people who wanted to travel to Ipswich or Bentley Station, or who wished to make a special journey. Billie's pony and that of his father were often put on Church Green to graze, and this kept the grass short and green.

Miller — Mr Hector Stone owned the mill which he had inherited from his uncle and aunt, Mr and Mrs H. Beckwith. He lived in the mill house with his sister, Miss Ruby Stone. The only power used originally was the river water which turned the water wheel that drove the round flat mill stones, grinding the corn into flour or meal for animal feed. By the time I knew about it, ten pairs of rollers had been fixed and a Crossley gas engine installed. This, with the help of some water power, drove the rollers which made the flour, and the stones that ground the corn into animal feed. The output of flour was about two tons in a twelve hour day, and three men and a boy were employed in the mill. In addition, three men worked as carters and general labourers. It was to Mr Stone's credit that bakers would buy his special wholemeal in preference to that sold by the bigger millers in Ipswich. In 1914 I started work in the mill and soon learned the secret of the wholemeal. It was simply the flour taken from the husk of the wheat, and the 'pollard' (part of the husk) mixed together on the floor with wooden shovels, and then bagged up and labelled 'Wholemeal'. I do not think the bakers ever knew how it was made. Some of the Wheat was supplied by local farmers, but as home-grown wheat was too soft to process by itself, a high proportion of Canadian Wheat was used. This came by train to Bentley Station. Mr A. Woollard, who was the licensee of the Bentley Tavern public house, contracted to cart the wheat to the mill with a two-horse-van, making two journeys a day. At the end of World War One the premises were extended, so that a much bigger output could be achieved. The expansion plan included the purchase of two Garrett Steam Wagons, and the erection of a jetty at Lower Holbrook to which sailing barges brought supplies of wheat from Canada and other places. To find a market for the extra tonnage, a full time traveller was engaged and, of course, extra employees to deliver the goods. This proved to be very costly, and led to the closure of the mill in 1926, and no flour has been made there since that date.

Shopkeepers — Mr James Munnings ('Scrivener') kept the little sweet shop at the top of East Row, and by the time I knew him he was quite an old man and was not very interested in hygiene. When one of the few lads who had any pocket money went to the shop for sweets, the transaction went something like this: "A pen'worth of aniseed balls, please." "How'd yer fist then — one, one, one and one, now how'd the tother." As the price was sixteen for a penny it meant four fists full! Scrivener caused quite a lot of good humoured fun in the last few years of his life, and passed on in 1907.

The Holbrook Branch of the Ipswich Co-operative Society was increasing its business at the beginning of the Century, and in 1907 two cottages and a piece of land which adjoined their property were purchased. The cottages were demolished and a much larger shop was built, which has been in operation ever since. At that time bread was baked on the premises and delivered by horse-drawn vans to several villages in the area. Mr Jack Thurston's father was the last man to bake bread there. Coal and paraffin oil were also delivered to some villages. The coal was brought from Ipswich or Bentley Station in the summer and stored in the yard. It was then weighed and sold by retail by a local man with a horse and van. Altogether seven men and one boy were employed, and four van horses were kept.

The Post Office and attached Stores were owned by Mr O. Kerridge, who retired in about 1906, when his son, Charles, took over the business and carried on for several years. The letters for the first delivery came by pony trap from Ipswich, and arrived at 5.30 a.m. The same conveyance called for the last collection at about 7.45 p.m., the pony having been stabled at Tattingstone in between the two journeys. The delivery of letters etc. was carried out by two local postmen, Mr Thomas Rowe and Mr Fred Rogers, who both continued until they reached retirement age. Mr Rowe's round started at the top of Fir Hill, and included every dwelling in Lower Holbrook and Harkstead, in the morning, and he made the first collection from Harkstead Post Office through Lower Holbrook at about 10 a.m., blowing a whistle as he proceeded. In the afternoon he again delivered to many houses in the same area, the exceptions being those dwellings which were off the beaten track. Both journeys were done on foot. Fred Rogers had a bicycle, and delivered to the greater part of the village in the morning. At mid-day he cycled to Bentley Station (calling at Stutton Post Office) with the first collection to put on the train for Ipswich. He then collected the second delivery from the 'up' train. On the return journey he again called at Stutton, and, after sorting the letters, proceeded to Holbrook, and did his second round. The road conditions were very bad, and this journey carried out six days a week, together with irregular meals, had an adverse effect on his health. At one time a swop of duties was arranged, but he bravely carried on until his retirement. Both postmen did morning deliveries seven mornings a week, unless a casual worker could be found who would take on the Sunday duty once a fortnight. The Christmas rush was a one day affair. The few Christmas cards and letters were all delivered on Christmas Morning, perhaps extending into the afternoon. The postmen usually had two casual workers to help them, and on Boxing Day they called at all the big houses for their annual tips. Then it started all over again. Postmen at that time were among the few workers that were given an annual holiday. I believe this was ten, or maybe fourteen days.

Shoe Makers and Repairers — Mr David Marjoram had a small workshop attached to his house in the Street, at the entrance to the Heath Field. As well as repairing all types of boots and shoes, he made heavy boots for the farm workers. These were all hand-stitched, and had hob nails and plates on the soles and heels. The customer would come to his shop in the early summer to be measured and give details, such as the length of the 'uppers', the number of lace holes, and if it was to be one or two tongues. In most cases the boots would be ready for collection at the end of August, and would be paid for out of the customer's harvest money, or, failing this, a shilling a week would be paid until the purchase was completed. The price was 13/- (a farm labourer's weekly wage). Mr Marjoram also sold new footwear, and hired out cycles, which he stored in a room at the front of the house.

At Holly Cottage, Mr D. Smith had a repair shop and specialized in stitching ladies' boots and shoes. He was quite an old man, and as his memory was failing, was unable to remember which customer's shoes were ready for collection. When he had finished repairing a pair of shoes, he carefully wrapped them up in brown paper, wrote the name of the owner on the parcel, and placed the same on a high shelf to await collection. When the customer called, 'Dod', as he was known to the villagers, proceeded to take the parcels off the shelf one by one until he found the right name. Sometimes this resulted in six or seven pairs of shoes being taken from the shelf and replaced. The boys of the village were quick to see this as an opportunity for a little fun, and often knocked on the door, and asked for someone's shoes, which they knew were not there. After taking down every parcel and then replacing them, the old chap would say, "Sorry, they are not finished. They will be done tomorrow!"

Veterinary Surgeon — Mr John Simson lived at Otter House, and travelled all over the Shotley Peninsula, attending to sick animals, large and small. He had inherited this practice from his father, and carried on the business until the outbreak of World War One: During the last few years he lived and practised at Hither House.

Relieving Officer — Holbrook was fortunate in having a Registrar of Births and Deaths, and the Relieving Officer living at Garland Cottage. This saved the parishioners a long journey to report a birth or death. Mr J. G. Francis, affectionately known as 'J.G.' travelled to all the villages in East Samford by pony and trap, paying relief money to the very poor and issuing Birth and Death Certificates. Once a month he attended the meeting of the Board of Guardians held at Tattingstone Workhouse. 'J.G.' was well known and respected in the village, and was a keen steel quoit player. He had an office in his house, and the iron entrance gate is still to be seen. As a boy I remember seeing tramps calling at the office to get a ticket for a night's lodging at Tattingstone Workhouse. They would arrive between three and four o'clock in the afternoon, having walked from Heathfields, Ipswich, and then had to walk the three miles to Tattingstone. Mr Francis died in 1911, and after that his duties were carried out by a Mr Alexander who lived at Capel and was already Registrar for West Samford. Mr Alexander visited the village fortnightly, and used the Reading Room as an office. Anyone requiring a certificate at any other time would have to travel to Capel St. Mary.

Insurance Agent — Mr J. W. Ward was agent for the Prudential Assurance Company, and also repaired cycles. He lived in the Street in the cottage now occupied by Mr and Mrs E. Hughes. In 1910 he moved into Sunny Side on the Heath, and carried on his business until he reached retirement age. His widow by a second marriage still lives in the same house.

Thatcher — Mr William Smith, better known as 'Hankey', lived at the Cherry Grounds, and in the summer he thatched stacks of hay and corn for the smaller farmers and small-holders. At other times of the year he did general repairs to wooden fences etc. His wife, Sally, was one of the few women who worked on the land.

Chimney Sweep — At Lower Holbrook we had a first-class chimney sweep in the person of Mr Robert Quantrill, who also did a bit of rabbiting, fishing, and shooting of wild fowls. He was the father of a very large family. His family was engaged in a variety of occupations and became well-known in the county. Mr Norman Quantrill of 'The Moorings' is one of the many grandchildren of Mr and Mrs Bob Quantrill.

Fishermen — At Lower Holbrook there also lived the joint owners of a fishing 'smack'. They would, when tide and wind permitted, travel up and down the river as far as Harwich, netting whatever fish were moving. On arrival at the 'Creek' the catch would be divided, and Mr Joe Dawson would walk to Harkstead and sell his share to the villagers. Mr Harry Spink would bring his basketful to Holbrook, and mostly found a ready market for everything he had. The price of a string of plaice or flounders was sixpence, with a charge of twopence for cleaning. If trade was slow he would offer to clean them free of charge. Mr William Sawyer of Clench Road, is one of his grandchildren.

Hawker — Last, but by no means least of the self-employed, was Charlie Quantrill, 'Boxer', who had a horse and covered van and travelled the locality selling paraffin oil, soap, pots, pans, and many other household goods. This business was later acquired by Mr Ernest Abbott, who, with members of his family, carried on for over fifty years. The store shed and stable were attached to Vine Cottage at the top of Alton Green, until about 1933, after which the business was conducted from Brook Farm.

Residences — Included in the list of private residences were:—

The Woodlands — The Rodwell Family
The Croft (now 'The Cedars') — Col. D. M. Murray
Holbrook House — Mr Gifford Reade
The Branthams (now 'Holbrook Lodge') — Mrs W. Rodwell
The White House — Mr F. Wase
Rose Cottage — Miss Hempson
The Hollies — Let on short terms
Broom Hill — Mr O'Malley
The Rectory — Rev. Mitchell Carruthers

Domestic maids were kept at all these houses. In some cases, as many as three were employed. At most places gardeners and grooms were employed.

As a result of Holbrook being an Open Village there were several casual workers. I think it would be true to say that, including employers, self-employed, and employees, 155 men who lived in the village were getting a 'living', as well as about 20 boys and 25 women. There were at least 115 horses and ponies kept, and I do not think that life was altogether dull and dreary.

Chapter 3

SOUNDS AND NOISES

The view held by some people that life in the village was 'monotonously quiet' is a completely false one. On most days the 'putta-putta-put' of the gas engine at the mill could be heard from 6 a.m. until 6 p.m., and then at intervals throughout the day the pleasant ringing sound of the Blacksmith's hammer on the anvil could be heard by people in the near vicinity. When the wind was in the right direction the hooter or bell at Waterside Works could be heard distinctly. It sounded several times during the day, but at 7.45 a.m. people took special note of it as it was accepted as Greenwich time, and workmen would set their watches at the correct time. If the wind blew from the opposite direction, the hooter at Brantham Xylonite Works could be heard, as well as the roar of the trains going over Cattawade Bridges. If the clock on Stutton School was heard striking, it was considered a sure sign of rain approaching. In School Term time the bell at the village school could be heard at 8.45 a.m., 8.55 a.m., 1.45 p.m. and 1.55 p.m. reminding parents, as well as children, that it was time for lessons. One has to bear in mind the fact that very few cottagers had reliable time pieces, and so the schoolmaster was anxious to help the scholars arrive on time. At about 9 a.m. on five mornings a week the bugle of 'Dilla' Stiff could be heard, and at 11 a.m. Percy Abbott blew his whistle, and those people who required goods from Ipswich would give their order to one of these two carriers. Then there were the Church Bells, which were rung for each Service, every Sunday, and for practice for 1½ hours on a Monday evening. One of the bells was used to inform the Village of a death. It would toll at intervals of three minutes, for an hour. I believe it was three pulls for a man, two pulls for a woman, and one for a child. The 'death' bell was also tolled at the time of a burial. It began to toll about an hour before the time fixed for the Church Service. This was a signal for the villagers to draw blinds as a mark of respect for the deceased. On arrival of the cortege at the Church, the bell was silent until the end of the Service. It was then tolled until the procession reached the graveside.

The sound of horses' hooves on the picked stoned roads was

quite common, and sometimes very interesting: each horse or pony had a distinctive step, especially when trotting. The heavy horses which pulled the waggons loaded with corn etc. were often very attractive with their braid and brasses, and the teamster would be congratulated when he pulled up at The Compasses to give the horses a rest.

It was also very interesting to listen to the sounds that came from the fields where ploughing and other operations were in progress. The horses were guided by verbal instructions, as well as by reins, namely 'Cupee-wee' meant go to the left, 'Grr Wherr-ee' to the right, and the well known 'Whoa'a there' meant stop. If these instructions were not obeyed, they would be repeated in a loud throated shout, with a few choice words added!

As there were very few machines around, it was possible to hear the footsteps of the workmen with their heavy footwear, going to and from work. One pensioner (Abraham Stiff) who was bedridden, would guess, mostly correctly, who was passing his house, by the particular 'step'.

As each butcher killed, on the premises, the animals which supplied the meat for the shops, some very distressing noises were often heard. Pig killing probably caused the greatest concern, and as I lived near to the slaughterhouse at Reed House I have vivid memories of the piercing shrieks that could be heard at killing time. The mournful blare of the bullocks, and the continuous bleating of the sheep was sure evidence of their unnatural surroundings.

Quite frequently, in the autumn, a set of threshing tackle would pass through the Village making an indescribable din and noise. First came a 'Ransome' Steam Traction Engine, pulling a threshing box or drum, and then followed an Elevator or Straw Pitcher. All three vehicles had heavy iron wheels and were without any kind of springs. Anyone who has never witnessed such a procession cannot possibly imagine the interest and excitement that was created. The engine driver and the steersman rode on the engine, and a third man rode in the pony cart that followed the elevator. In addition to the loud rattling noise that was created, a tell-tale trail of bits of straw, chaff, and dirt was left from one farm to another. Later on, when the threshing box had been 'set' along side a corn stack, more pleasant humming sounds could be heard, as the grain was separated from the straw. If the corn being threshed was wheat, it would be conveyed in coomb sacks to Holbrook Mill to be ground into flour.

Chapter 4

ACTIVITIES, RELIGIOUS LIFE, AND OUTSTANDING EVENTS

The game of steel quoits was popular at the beginning of the century, and Holbrook could boast several very good players, among them, the schoolmaster and the relieving officer. Matches were played on Saturday afternoons with teams from neighbouring villages. There were also county competitions, which the Holbrook team won on one or two occasions. Several men and lads would meet for a practice on the School Meadow, every evening in the summer months. Unfortunately, some of the players could not compete in the matches, as they had to work all day on Saturdays.

A football club was formed in about 1909, and Mr H. Cousins of Red House Farm allowed the team to play on one of his meadows. The outbreak of war in 1914 caused the break-up of the Club, but it was restarted in 1919 under its original name of 'Holbrook Rovers'.

Miss Eva Rodwell of the 'Branthams', Lower Holbrook formed a Musical Band, and trained several village men to play such instruments as violins, bass violas and clarinets. On one occasion they were asked to perform at the local Horticultural Show, and their efforts were well received.

The Working Men's Club was well attended in the Reading Room. It was open six evenings a week at a charge of twopence per week, and lads of 14 years of age or over were allowed to join. It was managed by a Committee of six local men, one of whom was on duty each evening to keep order, which he did without any serious trouble.

There was nowhere for the girls of the village to meet for social purposes, the obvious reason being that they were all engaged in domestic service and were only allowed out on one afternoon and evening each week. Most of the married women were members of the Mother's Union, which met in the Iron Room in the grounds of the Rectory. A photograph taken in 1900 shows twenty women and ten young children present, as well as the Rector.

There was also a full and loyal team of bell ringers, who rang the church bells regularly.

In 1910 a Regatta was held down at the Creek, and became a regular event until the outbreak of World War One. Besides boating and swimming races, there were other sporting events on the foreshore, and the presence of 'Barkers and Thurstons' Fair made the event very attractive.

After the Samford Horticultural Show was discontinued following the Show on Wherstead Park in September 1907, Holbrook with Freston and Woolverstone organised an annual show of their own, and from 1910 Holbrook carried on separately. Most years the Show was held in the Rectory grounds, the chief reason being the possibility of displaying the exhibits of flowers and vegetables in the Iron Room, thus saving the expense of hiring a large tent. A large proportion of the inhabitants attended each year, and it could truthfully be described as a very happy social gathering.

Church services were held at the Parish Church at 11 a.m. and 6.30 p.m. every Sunday, with Holy Communion being celebrated at 8 a.m. once a month. The Sunday School met in the afternoon in the Voluntary School premises. There was also a Sunday School at Lower Holbrook, which met regularly in the Infants' School room. Mission Services were also held there. Other meetings connected with the Church were held in the Iron Room at the Rectory. At the Wesleyan Chapel the Sunday School met at 10 a.m., and a young people's service followed at 11 a.m. At 12 noon there was a Class Meeting for adults. Preaching Services were held at 2.30 p.m. and 6.30 p.m. These were conducted mostly by Ministers and Lay Preachers from Ipswich. The Minister in charge, who lived at Chelmondiston, and was also Chaplain to the boys of Ganges, conducted a service in the schoolroom on alternate Tuesday evenings, and a prayer meeting was held every Thursday evening. There was a friendly atmosphere between the members of the two congregations, and united meetings for prayer were often held. The Rector, Rev. M. Carruthers, was very popular in the Village, and this was clearly shown on the last Sunday of his ministry when many people attended both the morning and evening services.

There was a Corps of the Salvation Army at Lower Holbrook, and several men of the village were members, and played musical instruments. Besides holding regular meetings in their barracks at Brook House, they met every Sunday afternoon in the Street. After playing hymns and other items for about half an hour they would go in procession to Fir Hill and conduct an open air service, if the weather was favourable. If not, they returned to their headquarters.

One of my earliest memories is of the General Election in 1906. As Holbrook provided the Polling Station for Freston, Stutton, and Tattingstone, as well as the voters in the village, the school was closed for the day, and it gave the boys an opportunity to support the candidate of their choice. By mid-morning two groups were formed, and proceeded to march to and fro between the school and the Compasses.

The first group carried a blue flag and chanted:—

'Tariff Reform means work for all.
Work for all, work for all.
Tariff Reform means work for all,
So vote for Capt. Pretyman.'

The second group, which included my brother, Jim, and myself, carried a yellow flat, and their message was:—

'Yes, Tariff Reform means work for all.
Work for all, work for all.
Tariff Reform means work for all,
Chopping up sticks in the workhouse.'

This was followed by:—

'Vote, vote, vote for Lacey Everett.
Hit Old Pretyman in the eye.
Mr Everett is the man,
And we'll help all we can,
And we don't care a bit for the Blues.'

Capt. Pretyman of Orwell Park had been Member of Parliament for this area for several years, but following the trend in many parts of the country, the Liberals won the day, and great was the rejoicing in which we boys had a part. The reader may be surprised to learn that I was only six years old then, and may wonder how I came to be involved. The reason was a simple one. My mother had three other lively lads, two running, and the other one crawling on the floor, and so she would say to my brother, who was three years older than I, "You can go out to play, Jim, but take Warrie with you, and mind you look after him."And so it was that at a very early age I learned quite a lot, both good and bad, that was going on in the Village.

Another event that occurred at that time was the alteration to the road at the Mill Corner, and the building of a new archway under the road. We went there as often as possible to watch the men at work. The waterway from the Mill alongside 'Pilbury's' meadow was cleaned out at the same time, and the mud taken by wheelbarrow on to the meadow. I do not believe anything has been done to the waterway since.

About this time Holbrook had its first motorcar. Its owner was Doctor Mahon. The man who had previously been groom had to be a non-driving chauffeur and accompany the doctor to 'crank up' after every call. The coming of the motorcar probably caused the District Council to take notice of the dangerous situation at the Post Office corner. The boundary fence of 'The Cedars' property came almost to a point, and a car going in or out of the driveway had to stop and reverse to make the turning. Traffic going from the Ipswich Road into the Street, or vice versa, also found it very difficult. A few feet of the grounds of the Cedars were taken for road widening and the wooden fence and gate replaced by iron palisading, thereby making a great improvement to the corner.

About this time, Dr Carey, who lived at 'The Beeches', realized that the Waiting Room for his patients was very small, so he had the wooden building erected, which still stands in the grounds and is now used as a chalet. The Doctor now had a consulting room, a dispensary, and a fairly large waiting room, which was greatly appreciated by the villagers.

Chapter 5

SAD STORIES

One could continue writing of other good things that happened, but unfortunately there are sad stories that have to be told.

The first of these was the closure of the family butchers business carried on at Reed Hall. The owner, Mr Freeman Allen, who was a very keen businessman and had at one time been chairman of the Parish Council, became a victim of liquor, as also did his wife. Not only did this cost a lot of money, but Mr Allen's business ability deteriorated, which affected buying as well as selling. When I was about six years old he had to have treatment, and my father was one of the men who acted as night nurse. Mr Allen had a smaller shop at Stutton to which he moved and the one at Holbrook was closed for good. The youngest boy of the family was in the same class at school as I, and losing him under such sad circumstances made a very deep impression on my young mind.

Very soon after this, a girl of twelve years of age, Alice Smith died of pleurisy on May 14 1907. Her grandparents lived quite close to our home, and I saw quite a lot of her when she visited them. She was full of fun and energy, and I was therefore mystified when I was told that she had died.

Within a few months the village policeman (Mr Edward Johnson) was taken ill and in a short time died of Pneumonia, leaving a widow, three sons, and two daughters. I remember thinking how terrible to let a policeman die, but, of course, there was no Health Service in existence then, and very few people were admitted to hospital — the local doctors had to do the best they could. As far as I know very little was done to help Mrs Johnson, and she moved out of the police station into a very small cottage next door to us. The youngest boy was taken into a police orphanage. The next one in age was sent to an uncle in Canada, and in a few years all the family had followed him. I had a very pleasant surprise in July 1977 when the youngest son and a grandson came into Holbrook Churchyard and I was able to have a chat with them. It was wonderful to meet Alan after nearly seventy years.

The closing of the Infants School at Lower Holbrook was a big disappointment to the people of that area, as it meant that every child of five years of age and over had to walk the one and a half miles to and from school every day. As far as can be ascertained, the cost of running the school was met jointly by the Rector and Squire Berners of Woolverstone Hall.

Two well-respected people, Doctor and Mrs Mahon, decided to leave the village for reasons unknown to the writer. Their departure added to the list of changes which everyone wished had not happened.

Towards the end of 1907, the Rev. M. Carruthers decided to leave Holbrook, giving as the reason the heavy financial burden that he had to bear. He moved to Little Munden in Hertfordshire. The Rev. Carruthers had been a very good pastor, as well as an effective preacher, and he was greatly missed, not least by the children with whom he was very popular. On one occasion I was with four other boys standing outside the Post Office Stores wishing we had a penny to spend. The rector came out of the shop smiling cheerfully. As he passed us he put his hand kindly on one boy's head, saying "How are you this morning, George?" For once George was lost for words! We had been bird nesting and George had some eggs in his cap which, of course, were broken, and as the yokes ran down his face, the rector turned his head and quickly walked away. This was typical of him and explained why the children all loved him.

Altogether 1907 had been a sad year for the village and became a subject for conversation for a very long time.

In spite of all the good wishes for 1908, it soon became evident that the hopes of the village population were not to be fulfilled. The family of Mr and Mrs Walter Double of Church green were the first ones to experience sorrow. A boy of six years old was taken ill and quickly became worse and died. One of his sisters suffered the same fate. By this time the illness had been diagnosed as 'Diptheria' and, as the girl had been attending school, other children were affected. Very soon Mr and Mrs Charles Clark were to mourn the loss of a boy and a girl. Panic struck the village as several other children became ill, and the Rector, Rev. C. P. Heywood, arranged for the Iron Room at the Rectory to be used as an isolation hospital. A trained nurse was brought in, and two mothers who had young children suffering from the complaint lived in the temporary hospital and assisted in nursing the invalids. Fortunately there were no more deaths, but it was several weeks before it was certain that the epidemic was a thing of the past. The two girls who died were in the same class at school as myself, and I have always felt very thankful that I did not become a victim. However, it seems certain that I was a ‘carrier’, as my youngest brother, who was only three years old and therefore did not attend school, caught the fever and joined the group in the hospital, although I am glad to report that his stay was a short one.

Chapter 6

GOOD NEWS AND DEVELOPMENTS

It was during 1908 that the first Old Age Pensions were paid, the amount being five shillings a week, which represented a third of a farm labourer's wage. My grandmother, Mrs Hannah Page, who lived at Halesgrove Cottages, was one of the first to receive the pension, and I remember how gratified she was for that rather small sum.

After the owner of the little sweet shop, Mr James Munnings, died, 'Dilla' Stiff, hired the shop and sheds and ran his carriers business from these premises. He also put a greater variety of sweets and small articles on sale in the shop and generally brightened up the place. On the other side of the Street changes were taking place. The Ipswich Co-operative Society had bought a pair of cottages and a plot of land adjoining their property, and soon building began on a much bigger shop, which led to more business and the employment of two additional assistants. It is interesting to note that the building still stands, and is the centre of an ever-increasing amount of business. Mr Horace Fyson was the branch manager when this extension was carried out.

In 1909 a new house was built on land ajoining the wheelwright's shop, by the Wagstaff family for Mr William Rogers. This house was given the name 'Hill-Side'. Strange to relate this was the first house to be built in the village for twelve years, the last one being Jubilee House, built in 1897 which stands nearby. At this time my parents had a very serious problem. We were living in a thatched cottage with only two bedrooms, and with a family of five boys and two girls it was obvious that something had to be done. There were very few cottages with three bedrooms, and there was no council accommodation and my parents became very worried. In desperation they applied for, and obtained the licence of the White Horse Public House. We moved in during November 1909, and we boys were delighted. With four bedrooms we had plenty of space, but for Mother and Father it meant more work.

The need for three-bedroomed cottages was very great, and in 1910 Mr Gifford Reade sold part of the Heath Field to local people for building purposes. The first purchaser was Mr J. G. Francis, who had a pair of cottages built for letting. He had bought an acre of land and intended to build four more cottages, but unfortunately he died before this could be done. Mr F. Rogers and Mr H. Wagstaff co-operated and had two semi-detached houses built the same year. The next year Mr Thomas Rowe had a spacious detached house built on an acre of ground, and Mr H. Smith had a smaller house built on a ¼ acre of land, and Mr F. Phillips was responsible for having a row of ten cottages erected for letting.

One of the conditions of the land sale was that the strip of land to be used as a road should not be included in the area bought by each purchaser. This appeared to be a generous act on the part of Mr Reade, but it proved to be a mistake because no one owned the road, but all the property owners had the right to use it and, as no one was responsible for its upkeep, it soon became nothing but a mud track and remained so until about five years ago when the rest of the field was sold. A plot of land on the south side of the field was sold to the Rector, The Rev. M. Washington, who had a residence built for his curate. This house is now known as 'South Side'.

So following twelve years of stagnation, nineteen houses were built in three years. These were quickly occupied, some of them by tenants of the East Row cottages who had been overcrowded for many years. This period saw the beginning of the expansion of the village, which, with the exception of the War Years, has been going ever since.

Chapter 7

THE MYSTERY PLAGUE

Although the houses concerned were not strictly within the Parish boundary, everyone in the village was deeply disturbed when a mysterious illness broke out at Latimer Cottages in the summer of 1910. A Mr Chapman, his wife, and one of her daughters by a former marriage, were all taken very ill, and in a very short time all three died, as did also a Mrs Parker of Turkey Farm, who went into the house to help. Various suggestions were put forward then and since as to the cause of death, but it is not certain if any of these are correct.

One possible reason was given as poison carried by rats. Another that the family had eaten a rabbit affected by Myxomatosis. A third that the illness was brought from London. This third suggestion is, to my mind, the most feasible, as the farm on which Mr Chapman worked often had barge loads of 'muck' brought from London, and unloaded at Slumpy Lane Yard, and men taking part in this operation were quite likely to pick up an infection. This theory is supported by the fact that a similar outbreak occurred at Erwarton a few years later, and local doctors were of the opinion that the disease could be one and the same. The interesting thing is that the victims at Erwarton were wives of farm workers who worked on a farm that regularly received refuse from London in the same way.

It was natural that news of these deaths should spread around the area very quickly, and people became very concerned, so much so that rabbit pie was taken off the menu. There are still relatives of all the victims living in the locality and they all agree that it was a mystery.

Chapter 8

CHANGES

During 1910 other changes took place. Dilla Stiff had left the Little Shop and was now the licensee of the Compasses Inn. The carriers business which he later sold to Mr John Smith was operated there. The Little Shop was let to Mr Ernest Golding, who turned it into a pork butchers shop, and besides selling the products over the counter, he travelled the neighbouring villages with a pony cart. Unfortunately this venture did not succeed, and after a few months Mr J. Smith hired the shop and buildings, and once again the carriers business was carried on there.

The Rev. C. P. Heywood was compelled by ill-health to resign as Rector of the Parish, and in July 1910 the Rev. Marmaduke Washington came to the village as the new Rector.

At the end of the year, Mr and Mrs George Redding retired as Headmaster and Mistress of the village school, posts that they had held for twenty-seven years. During that long period they had won the respect and admiration of many people, and a special meeting was held in the Rectory Room to bid them farewell. A collection had previously been made and a present of £20 was given to them and an illuminated and framed address with the signatures of the school managers. Various gifts were contributed by the scholars of the school, and Mr Redding was presented with a beautiful umbrella by the members of the Working Men's Club, for which he had done valuable service. Before he retired, Mr Redding had photographs taken of all the scholars, with the five teachers in three groups. A copy of one of these groups is in my possession; it would be interesting to hear about the other two.

At the beginning of 1911, Mr and Mrs J. C. Young began their duties as Headmaster and Mistress of the village school, and in many ways change was the order of the day. This was to be expected but not always welcomed.

House building was increasing on the Heath Field, and this had two good results. Bigger cottages were available for letting and there was an increase in employment of skilled and casual labour. Most of the bricks being used were made at the Holbrook Brickworks, which was good for the village. Unfortunately these were not of the highest standard. Machinery had been installed to cut and dry the bricks, which often were soft and badly shapen and also contained an excess amount of salt. At the Wherstead Brickyard all the bricks were made by hand, and these were purchased by the builders and put in the front of the houses in order to give them a better appearance. All the bricks were transported by horsepower. The contractors were Mr Percy Abbott, Mr Tommy Smith, and Mr C. Earle, who had a pony, Tom by name, that refused to work with blinkers and always carried his head on one side. Charlie was a very strong man, and he had a rope attached to the cart so that when they came to a hill he could help Tom. Some people declared that he pulled as much as the pony.

The highlight of that year was the day of the Coronation of King George V and Queen Mary. The school children walked to Holbrook House and each received from Mr Reade a medal and refreshments. A service was held in the Parish Church at midday, and in the afternoon sports were held on the school meadow. This was followed by a tea and games. It was estimated that six hundred people attended the function.

Chapter 9

SCHOOL DAYS

I would now like to recall some memories and impressions of my school days, which began, so I have been told, when I was 3½ years old.

The Headmistress was the mother of five boys, and had a lot of sympathy for mothers of large families, so when my mother, who had two children younger than I, approached her she readily agreed to take me into the babies class. I cannot remember much of what happened in that class, but after I had been promoted to the infants,

Teachers and Scholars. Holbrook School. 1910.

Back row left to right — Thurnley Studd, Evelyn Studd, William Howes, Frank Bowles, Charlie Pepper, Cyril Smith, Fred Whittle, James Page, Warrie Page, George Marjoram, Albert Rush.

Second back row — Miss Plum, Miss Bevan, Miss E. Howard, Elsie Smith, Mary Porter, Nellie Rush, Florrie Smith, Ada Dunnett, Mabel Double, Annie Ridout, May Goodall, Miss E. Double, Mrs Redding, Mr G. Redding.

Second front row — Herbert Marjoram, Cecil Smith, Marjorie Smith, Millicent Smith, Muriel Abbott, Gwen Smith, May Codling, Violet Howlett, Eva Marjoram, Edward Hughes, Kenneth Page, Alice Codling.

Front row — Laurie Smith, Queenie Abbott, Wilfred Abbott, Denis Smith, Daisy Smith, Raymond Page, Phyllis Page, Millicent Studd, Frank Double, Dorothy Smith, Alice Marjoram, Reginald Page, Bert Ridout.

life became a little more interesting. I remember, quite clearly, the Headmistress being unwell one day and going home. One of the older girls, Priscilla Smith, was sent in to take charge of the class. A cardboard clock-face stood on a shelf, and Priscilla took this down and spent the whole afternoon teaching us to tell the time. We all enjoyed that lesson, and I am still wondering why the mistress had not done the same thing. Just before I was seven years old I was moved to another class. They were called 'Standards' in those days. I was put in 'Standard One', together with several others, including George Marjoram and Albert Rush. I mention this because the three of us kept together all our school days and always were good friends; we still are, although George lives in the south of the country and is unable to meet us for a chat.

We had a very good teacher in the person of Miss May Stannard, and she gave us a good grounding in the '3 R's', and the basic elements of education. Old scholars of Miss Stannard all have one thing in common — a vivid memory of her right hand with which she meted out punishment when necessary. A good slap by that right hand on one's face was not likely to be forgotten for a very long time. On one occasion Miss Stannard was helping a girl with her lessons. She was sitting in a row just in front of us boys and was wearing a blue serge pleated skirt. As she bent forward I very mischieviously followed, at a safe distance, the line of one of the pleats. Albert gave my elbow a sharp jolt and, quick as lightning, May's right hand landed on George's face, followed by "Take that, my boy!"

Apart from the incident just mentioned, George, Albert and myself did not get into any serious trouble while we were in Standards 1 and 2, but when we reached Standard 3 we ran into trouble. In those days the 3rd Standard was very much like the Eleven Plus. There were tests to be taken and if these were not passed it meant staying in this class for another year. It was then that we caught up with Walter Southgate, who was beginning his second year, and Ted Smith who was entering his third, which fact speaks for itself. I think Walter would probably have fitted in nicely with our little group, but Ted was a very different proposition. He had neither the mental ability nor the inclination to concentrate on any kind of work. Whatever the lesson he would seriously consider it for about ten minutes, during which time he would knit his brows and scratch his head several times, and then suddenly take his pencil up, scribble something down, and then abandon it as a bad job. As a result of this, while we were trying to solve a problem Ted was thinking up a tormenting trick to play, all the time cleverly keeping out of sight of the teacher. That was in the days of long benches, with five scholars to a bench. Somehow or other Ted always managed to sit in the middle, and quite often managed to get one of us into trouble. Strangely enough we never resented his trick playing, probably because he was such a likeable lad and never showed any signs of bad temper. It would take a very long time to recall all the punishments that Ted was responsible for, but I will give the facts of three separate incidents, the first of which I had a part in.

As Mr Redding was getting near to the age of retirement he delegated the physical training lesson to the other teachers, and on one particular day our teacher, Miss Davies, was in charge, and we were assembled on the girls' playground, facing south and back to the school buildings. There were three holes in the ground, about the size of a saucer and as deep as a cup, which the girls used for some kind of ball game. On this particular morning the holes were full of water. Miss Davies was in the habit of taking a step backward every time she gave a one, two order, and Ted, who was always alert for a bit of fun, noticed that she was getting nearer to one of these holes. So, keeping cautiously behind the girl in the front row, he turned his head towards me and said, "She's going in that hole in a minute." And sure enough it happened, and Miss Davies had great difficulty in regaining her balance, which we both thought was a great joke. Ted stood perfectly upright to give vent to his feelings, but I stooped down to be, as I thought, unseen. Just then there was a sharp tap on the window, and a guilty conscience made me turn to look. Mr Redding beckoned me into his room. His words are still very clear in my mind. "Warrenton," he said, "I've never had to cane you before, and I'm very sorry to have to do so now." The thought passed through my mind that he really was not obliged to, so I had one stroke of the cane and joined the group again, taking my place beside Ted who was quite evidently enjoying the whole episode.

It was Walter's turn next to be Ted's victim. As our class was overcrowded an extra bench had been brought in and placed against a wall at right-angles to, and facing the other four benches, with a narrow gangway between. One day when Ted was making a general nuisance of himself, Miss Davies moved him to the end of one of the other benches. Ted responded by turning in his seat and leaning his slate on the front of our desk, from which position he could still cause a lot of trouble. Twice that day the teacher rushed down the gangway and cracked Ted's knuckles with a sharp edge of a 12 in. ruler. She tried a third time, but Ted was too quick, and as he smartly drew his hands away, the ruler cracked on to the slate, which fell to the floor with a loud rattle, disturbing the other two classes in the room, as well as our own. This really infuriated the teacher, and she promptly moved Ted to the other end of the bench, where he was surrounded by girls with whom he was no favourite, and I suppose Miss Davies thought he would be safe there. Ted did behave himself for the rest of that day, but the next morning he yielded to temptation again, and as everyone else was working in complete silence, a heavy thud was heard, and then a quick rustle, followed by a second heavy thud. Ted had thrown a heavy book over the heads of four girls and it had landed on Walter's face, who, as quick as lightning, had returned it. Ted, of course, dodged it, and it hit a girl in the next class. Then the real trouble began; Walter was ordered into the Headmaster's room, but refused to go because Ted threw the book first. The teacher would not hear anything about that. She evidently was only prepared to believe what she saw, "Southgate, I saw you throw the book, and you are to go to Mr Redding," but Walter stayed put. Just before break-time another attempt was made to solve the problem. "Southgate, are you going in to Mr Redding?" "Yes, if you send Ted Smith with me." This the teacher refused to do, so it was back to square one. I said in a loud whisper, "I don't blame you, Walter." "You stay in as well Page," demanded Miss Davies. Albert mumbled something about it not being fair, and again the teacher's high pitched voice sounded, "You stay in Rush with them." So the three of us remained in our seats as the rest of the class proceeded to the playground, and as Ted was going through the doorway he turned and gave us a most tantalizing grin. With all the other scholars out of the way Miss Davies tried again. "I'll give you another chance," she said, "Will you go in to Mr Redding?" Walter replied, "You've let Ted Smith go out to play and I'm not going without him." The teacher then went to the sliding door at the other end of the room, and as she put her head through the opening, Walter said to me, "Let me come," and he went out by the back door, and ran through the playground and continued on until he reached his home at Park Cottages. The Headmaster sent one of the older boys to fetch him back, which he was able to do without any trouble. Walter told his story to the Master who must have accepted it, because Walter was not punished, and in a very short while we had a new teacher.

Within a few weeks all Standard 3 children were put into Standard 4, which was supervised by the Headmaster. As Mr Redding had recently retired we found ourselves in the hands of a new and very harsh master in the person of Mr John Young. We very soon learned that even minor offences were punished by a very heavy stroke of the cane on the left hand. As the right hand was never caned there was no excuse for not working. Ted was still with us, and although he knew how strict Mr Young was he just could not resist the temptation to indulge in trouble-making. Arithmetic was the worst of Ted's subjects and if he got two sums correct out of six it was quite certain he had copied, and those of us who sat close to him were blamed for letting him copy. One morning when we were struggling with divisions and fractions with our elbows up to prevent Ted getting a peep, trouble started again. There was dead silence throughout the room when everyone was startled by a terrible scream. Mr Young shouted, "Come out the boy who made a noise like a chicken." Out walks Albert. "What did you make that hideous noise for?" "Please Sir, Ted Smith nipped me." "Come out here Smith," commanded Mr Young, who then proceeded to give both boys a very heavy stroke with the cane. As they came back to their desk, Ted whispered to Albert, "Don't howl, don't howl." Poor Albert, he was treated as if he was the culprit, instead of the victim in this piece of horse play. But this was not uncommon with this master, who tried to solve every problem with his beloved cane.

One of the changes that Mr Young made as soon as he had taken charge of the school was to cut the bell ringing down to a minimum. Instead of a long ring at a quarter and five minutes to nine, Mr Young gave the bell three sharp pulls, as he entered the school at two minutes to nine, and then walked briskly to his room. He then put his books on the desk, walked through to the lobby door, marshalled the boys who were there and quickly got them into school. He shut the door and every boy who was late received the appropriate punishment. Another habit of his was to creep out of the room when we were all busy and stay out for quite a long time, long enough in fact for some of the scholars to indulge in paper pellet throwing, jeering, and sometimes fighting. Eventually Mr Young would return very quietly, and when the uproar had subsided he would call out a few names and direct them to his desk. He then reached for his cane and gave each boy a sharp stroke of the cane on the left hand. We often wondered how he knew who the culprits were. One of the smart girls discovered the secret and passed it on to the boys. The makers of 'Bovril' had organised a big advertising scheme. Special coupons were put on the top of each bottle, and anyone collecting a certain number of these coupons could obtain a large sized picture. Mr Young got all the children interested in this, and persuaded them to bring the coupons to school. The response was so good that he was able to get three really good pictures, which certainly improved the look of the room. We learned to our dismay that these pictures served a dual purpose; they were hung in such a way as to act as mirrors, and every time the master left the room he made sure the door was not closed, and so, looking through the small opening into a picture, he could see everything that was going on. We never really forgave him for that. I have wondered since how many poor mothers bought Bovril that they could ill afford, so that the child could take one of those coupons to school.

Another of Mr Young's tricks was to hook the handle of his cane on to his braces at the back and then with both hands free he would walk very quickly between the desks, looking for anything that was not strictly connected with the lesson, such as drawings of animals, or messages to other scholars. When a culprit was detected the cane would be taken from its hanging and two or three very sharp strokes would be administered on the shoulders of the offending boy or girl. When this happened the whole class was terrified, and no one dare look up, lest they should suffer the same fate. Being comparatively young and very nimble, he was able to move around so very quietly that quite often no one knew where he was, with the result that everyone had a very uneasy feeling that they were being watched. It was not surprising that within a few weeks a great change had taken place. Mr Young could leave the room for fifteen or twenty minutes without there being any sign of disorder, and I'm sure our work was the better for it, but it must be said that it was 'obedience through fear rather than out of respect'.

One of the good things that Mr Young did for Holbrook School was to start gardening classes for the older boys. There were six plots, with two boys to each, and these lessons were both instructive and enjoyable. They were also rewarding because the boys were allowed to have some of the produce. Alas, this privilege led to trouble when a boy who was leaving school the next day asked it he could have some broccoli. He was told that this was not ready for cutting and therefore he could not take any. Needless to say, he was rather peeved about this refusal. The Church of England Sunday School met in the Day School premises, and the next Sunday afternoon after Sunday School the boy persuaded other boys to follow him into the garden and cut the heads off every broccoli. They were seen by the Master's wife, and the next morning the Master lined the boys up and gave each one a heavy stroke of the cane, from the oldest to the youngest, who was about nine years old. The irony of this was that the ring leader got off scot free as he had left school for good.

In writing about these canings I would like to make it clear that I had no personal grievance against Mr Young. I can only remember two occasions when I received punishment, and then I deserved it. To the best of my knowledge neither of my two chums, George and Albert, nor myself were caned after the first six months with our new master. I think there were three reasons for this, the first one being that Ted Smith had left school. Another reason was that we had learned from other boys' mistakes. Some were sullen, some stubborn, others refused to work, and the younger ones were too nervous to hold out a hand for the cane and so they were thrashed on any part of the body available. The best policy to follow if one was accused of an offence, whether guilty or not, was to walk to the Master's desk, hold out the left hand, close your eyes and grit your teeth, and then walk quietly back to your desk, making a desperate effort to keep the tears back and carry on with the lesson as if nothing had happened. The third reason was probably the best. Mr Young instituted what was known as silent reading. Every morning the book monitor had to place on the shelf under each desk a reading book. Every boy and girl had a copy of the same one. At one time it was 'Treasure Island'. The instruction was that the story book had to be taken out and read directly any lesson was finished, and the industrious scholars soon became interested in the tale. I'm sure Jim Hawkins & Co. kept us very often out of trouble!

The incident I am about to relate was the worst thing I witnessed during my school days. There was a family of two boys and a girl who attended the school, the girl being the youngest. One day the mother kept the girl from school, took her to Ipswich shopping, and for reasons best known to herself, did not inform the teacher. The registers were brought as usual into the Headmaster, and noting that the girl was absent, inquired of the older boy the reason. The dialogue went something like this: "Why isn't your sister at school, Cousins?" "Don't know, Sir." "Is she ill?" "Don't know, Sir." "What do you mean, 'don't know'?" "I don't live with my parents, Sir." "Where do you live then?" "With my grandparents, Sir." The master became infuriated and sent for the younger brother, who was in another room. He came in very timidly and was confronted by the same question, "Why isn't your sister at school?" "Don't know, Sir," and with that the master completely lost control of his temper. He took hold of the boy with his left hand, and proceeded to hit him with the cane until the boy fell on the floor exhausted. There were about forty scholars in the room, all older than this unfortunate boy, and we were all too frightened to move. I have had a guilty conscience about this all my life as I feel we should never have allowed an innocent boy suffer as he did. The father came to the school during a lunchtime and threatened to thrash the master, but as the master kept strictly on school premises nothing came of it. We older boys hoped it would be reported to the police, so that we would be given the opportunity to say what happened, but we never heard a word more, and from that time we formed the opinion that the master, the school governors, the police, and even some of our parents, were 'ganged' up against us, and that nobody was on our side. The statement by the chairman of the governors at the time of Mr and Mrs Young's departure from the village gives support to this idea. Quote, "Our day schools are sustaining a great loss in the removal of Mr and Mrs Young. We shall miss them much in school and parish. Our school has greatly benefited by their teaching, musical instruction, and wise control." It is very doubtful if even one senior scholar agreed with that last phrase. 'Harsh control' would have been more appropriate. If Mr Young had been able to control his temper, as well as he controlled his pupils, he would have been a first-class teacher.

The reference to the musical instruction was certainly correct. By the end of their first year at Holbrook, Mr and Mrs Young had organized a school concert, the first of its kind. This was given in the two large rooms at the school, which were not very suitable for such an event. The wood and glass partition at one end was opened, and the stage erected so that half was in one room, and half in the other. The audience was divided in the same way so that only half of the performers could be seen. Every class in the school took part, and at each evening performance every seat was occupied. The profit of £5.00 was used to buy a piano, something the school had never possessed. A second concert was arranged about a year later. This was given in the Iron Room at the Rectory, which was much more suitable. Again the programme, which was presented twice, was greatly appreciated, the one regrettable fact being the failure of the senior scholars to do what was expected of them. What should have been the opening chorus had to be cancelled, because we persisted in being 'flat' at rehearsals. The song was about a jolly fiddler, but the tune did not catch on, and we never really became interested. Another item that suffered the same fate was a Dutch action song. It was composed for girls and boys in Dutch costumes to sing and dance, but the boys were not very enthusiastic. I think if we had been allowed to choose our own partners it would have been more successful! The fact that this event was such a success was due to the very efficient way in which the younger children did their parts, especially the primary class, of whom my younger sister who was three years old was a member. Great credit was due to Mr Young who was chiefly responsible for the programme, especially when one remembers that he was his own pianist, as he courageously persevered with training the four senior classes in the school. The time soon came for Mr and Mrs Young to move on to their next appointment at Southend, and we boys were very anxious about the manner and methods of our future head. Of one thing we were certain, if we did get into any kind of trouble we would not be punished with the same cane. Six of us had retrieved that weapon from its resting place, cut it up into twelve pieces and put one piece each in our pockets. We then proceeded to smoke the other pieces, and needless to say, we soon began to feel sick. Our fears were groundless as Mr Gribble's attitude was very different. In the nine months that I remained at school I saw the cane used only once.

Chapter 10

LIFE OUT OF SCHOOL HOURS

During the winter months there was very little for children to do on Saturdays and during school holidays. Shortage of clothes was one of the difficulties that parents had to contend with. If the youngsters were out in the rain there would be no change of clothes for them when they got back to their homes. The roads were rough and muddy, with plenty of pools of water, and the most sensible thing for mothers to do was to keep the younger children at home. For the large families living in very small houses, this meant quarrels, grumbles, and fights. Boys particularly disliked this confinement, and often shoes were hidden to prevent them from going outside. No wonder mothers prayed for fine weather!

Some of the older boys were allowed to go to the farms and join the men in the barns, looking after the cattle and pigs, but usually only two boys were allowed in one shed, with strict instructions to behave themselves.

With the arrival of spring, life became a bit more interesting for the children, and a little easier for the mothers, who were glad to have more room in which to do the housework. It has to be remembered that the village itself was very small, extending from the Church to the School, and from the Post Office to the butchers shop on Ipswich Road, but the present day playing field at the junior school was available for the children and many hours of fun and games were spent there. In the afternoons some of the mothers would join the boys and girls. Older children often went to Fir Tree Hill, which was then an open space and considered by most people to be common land. With plenty of trees giving shade in the summer-time, and grassy banks and slopes, it made an ideal playground. As it was a considerable distance from most of the houses it sometimes meant being late home for meals.

I remember winters when the Fish Pond was frozen, and the ice thick enough for sliding and skating, and then, of course, it was fun for the youngsters and anxiety for the parents — "You be careful." "Don't you go out far," and, "Be sure to be home at five for tea."

These were some of the instructions given to reckless boys who were not supposed to be on the ice unless an adult was there.

A lot of children had to use the roadway between the Compasses and the Co-op shop as a playground, and in the very dark evenings during November and December they would play hide and seek, making the back entrance to 'East Row' (or as we knew it 'Barrack Row') 'Home'. The only light to be seen was from the Co-op shop, and so there were many hiding places in dark alleys and corners, and seeking was a very skilful job. The fact that children could leave school at the age of 13 years, and the availability of part-time work, greatly reduced the numbers of youngsters who were to be found in the street.

Some boys would work at one of the big houses for an hour in the morning, and for the same period in the afternoon, and often all day on Saturday. Girls were mostly kept busy helping their own mother or a neighbour or friend, and either a boy or girl of every family had to fetch milk from the nearest farm every morning before going to school. I myself had four part-time jobs before I left school, earning from eighteen pence to three shillings a week, of which Mother was glad to have two shillings to help with the housekeeping. I had to put sixpence into the school bank for clothes, leaving sixpence for myself.

One of my part-time jobs was at Broom Hill, where, in addition to fetching milk, chopping sticks, getting in coal, cleaning shoes and cutlery, I had to pump water to fill the tanks at the top of the house. The big iron force pump stood in the kitchen, and I had to stand on a box to reach the handle. The occupant of the house at that time was an actress who spent a lot of her time in hotels, and was in the habit of taking a bath each morning. This lady had no idea of the number of strokes of the pump that were needed to fill the supply tank, and very often the water did not run out of the overflow pipe, for at least five days, and, of course, it could have been dangerous if the hot water system had run dry. I was due at school at 9 a.m., and very often at about 8.30 a.m. one of the maids would kindly suggest that I went for my breakfast, adding that if the water got low during the day she would give a few strokes of the pump to save trouble. By this time I was famished, and thankfully ran home to breakfast, and later ran to school. Had it not been for the kind consideration shown by that young woman, I should probably have gone hungry to school.

During the last summer school holiday that Bob Simpson and I had, we helped to get the harvest in at Red House Farm on the Woodlands Estate. The farmer at that time was a Mr Henry Cousins, who was always willing to allow boys on his farm, providing they were willing to work. So Bob and myself very soon set about helping the three harvesters cut and cart the corn. The farmer encouraged us to work well, by telling us "You're a couple of good boys. I'll give you a Golden Sovereign after harvest." The men were greatly amused by this promise and often reminded us of it. Every morning after finishing my part-time job and having my breakfast, we joined the three men in whatever kind of work they were engaged in, and stayed with them all day long until seven in the evening. We were thirteen years old then, and quite strong. So between us we did as much work as an extra man. We enjoyed loading and unloading the wagons, and were quite happy, and our parents did not have to worry about us getting into mischief. I think the Royal Mint must have been short of gold that year, because we never got our Sovereigns! However, we were not surprised or offended, in fact, we should have been very surprised if the promise had been kept. Of course, the men teased us in a good natured way, and we accepted this as a good joke for many years.

During the harvest holidays more part-time jobs were available, and boys were hunting round for them long before the holidays started. Often fathers could get jobs for their sons at the place of their employment, although this was sometimes a disadvantage as the

Fir Tree Hill. Holbrook

boss would report any misbehaviour to the father who was expected to mete out punishment.

The Fish Pond was a regular attraction, and many happy hours have been spent in fishing from the road side, and exploring along the meadow side. The wooded side was strictly out of bounds, as it was part of Squire Berner's favourite pleasure ground. Of special interest was the small archway at the foot of Fir Tree Hill, through which the surplus water flowed on its way via the meadows to Holbrook Creek. A favourite pastime was to remove a board from the entrance to the archway, thereby letting the water run very quickly through for about fifteen minutes, by which time it was hoped that a good number of eels had been washed through. The board was then replaced, and a search began from the other side of the road, and if an eel was spotted a great deal of fun was enjoyed in trying to catch it. On one occasion a large number of eels were found in the archway, and two of the older boys crawled in, caught some of them, and handed them to those of us who stood at the entrance. When the two boys came out they were very annoyed because we hadn't any eels, but when we showed them the sixpence that a woman had paid for them, their attitude changed and we all quickly made our way to the Little Sweet Shop. This operation had to be carried out with great care, and one boy was always posted on the road to raise the alarm if anyone was approaching, particularly the gamekeeper who always kept a sharp look out for trespassers. On one of our exploring visits in the archway, we discovered that it was built in two parts, which seemed to prove the truth of the story that had been told, namely that at one time it was a footpath only, and then the archway was lengthened and the bank made wider and higher so that a road could be constructed for vehicles to travel on between Holbrook and Lower Holbrook.

During school holidays many happy hours were spent at 'The Creek', or as it was known then, 'The Shore'. However, owing to the danger element, we were not allowed to go there without an adult with us. On a Whit Monday my older brother and myself were allowed to go with the mother of another boy, and after we had enjoyed ourselves in the water and as the tide went down, we joined some boys from Lower Holbrook who were playing in a boat anchored nearby. After a while our guardian reminded us that some children who lived at Lower Holbrook had been ill with Chicken Pox, and she suggested that we get into another boat anchored a little way off. What she did not know was that there were fishing nets on the seats of the boats. Two days later our police sergeant met me in the New Cut, and in an official and frightening voice asked, "Were you down at the Creek on Monday?" "Yes, Sir," I replied. "Did you know you damaged some fishing nets?" he went on. "No, Sir," I said. He carried on, "Well you did, and you had better go to see Mr Quantrill and find out what he is going to do about it." Needless to say I was very frightened as this six foot three man in blue looked very sternly down at me — four feet nothing. It so happened that I did not have to go to Mr Quantrill, as our parents decided that my brother and his pal, who were three years older than myself and George who was with us, should go and convince Mr Quantrill that it was unintentional, and that we were all very sorry. We were all very pleased that our apology was accepted, and if we were willing to pay for the time that it took to repair the nets Mr Quantrill would be satisfied. So we paid one shilling each, and felt very thankful we had got off so lightly.

The manager of the Co-op Stores kept a Collie dog, named Rover, who was friendly with the boys of the village. One day, four of us had taken Rover for a walk, and as we walked through a meadow a rabbit was disturbed. Rover gave chase and caught it. Having killed the rabbit, the next problem was what to do with it, as we realized it was not fit for human consumption. At that moment a man came along in a pony cart. We stopped him and asked if he would buy our catch. After a good look he said he would take it for his ferrets, and gave us tuppence. We were delighted, and very quickly made our way to the sweet shop.

Holbrook, in common with many other villages, had some very interesting and noteworthy residents, one of whom was Alfred Hadley. I remember Alfred more for the things he did not do, than for any special thing that he did! He **never** tied his boot laces up, even when he walked to his allotment which was below the Church. He **never** shut the back door to his house, but always tied it with a six inch opening for the cats, and he **never** pulled down the roller blind to his window, which made it easy for us to watch him reading the 'Evening Star' while the cats helped themselves to the butter on the table. He lived in a wooden cottage at the back of the Co-op Shop, and one of his regular grievances was that he did not get 'Divi' on his rent money, and as he paid it at the local shop a good many people enjoyed a good laugh as he argued with the manager. Then there was Bob Driver, who at one time kept a donkey in a shed at No. 2 Barrack Row, and did a bit of dealing. He was crippled with rheumatism and in his latter years very seldom went further than the Wesleyan Chapel where he played a concertina which was very often out of tune with the organ. Ben Scott, who in his younger days had been a brickmaker, was now the school master's gardener, and also kept the churchyard tidy. Ben was a favourite with the younger children. Apparently he had reached his second childhood rather earlier in life than most people, and on the way to school would take children by the hand and give them 'jumps'. Of course, he was soon surrounded by boys and girls chanting, "Give me a jump, please Mr Scott." Amos Leeks was the local roadman, and with his wheel-barrow, pickaxe and shovel, tried to keep the roads in good order. He was a very wise workman, which was apparent from the fact that he carried his shovel with him wherever he went. At whatever part of the village he was working he allowed time to walk to his house by leaving off time, and, of course, as he was carrying his shovel no one could accuse him of leaving off too soon. Another man who will always be remembered by my generation was Dilly Dunnett who, with his wife and large family, lived at No. 3 Barrack Row. Dilly tried hard to make people believe that he had his children well under control, and had a habit of talking with a tone of authority in his voice. In the summer evenings he would come into the road and command his boys and girls to go to bed at once. The roll call followed this patter: "Purs, Poll, Lawer, George, Elsie, Bedtime — indoors at once." Then in answer to a query from an onlooker as to whether they were all there, he would answer, "I'd better go in and count them," and as he went in at the back door the two boys would come out through the front door, to the great delight of their pals, who then encouraged them to keep out until it got dark. On one Guy Fawkes evening the boys placed a lighted candle on the chopping block and were having great fun with all the other lads letting off fireworks when Dilly appeared in a bad temper. He took the candle and went indoors again. For a time all was quiet, and then one of the bright boys noticed that the wooden doorstep between the two small rooms was worn away in the middle. So a large firework was placed under the door, and the next moment all three doors were opened to let the smoke out, and George took the opportunity of retrieving the candle. From then on the firework display continued without hindrance.

Chapter 11

HOME LIFE

The first home I remember was No. 1 Thatched Cottages, which was situated near to the Post Office and consisted of four small rooms with low ceilings and brick floors. This row of houses was built mainly of wood, with approximately eighteen inches of brickwork as a foundation. Wooden sills measuring approximately nine inches by four inches were laid on the brickwork and large wooden posts were fixed at each corner of the rooms. Smaller pieces of wood, known as Studs, were then fixed to the sills and beams at about fifteen inch intervals. Like most old houses the floors were below ground level, and there were two steps down at the back door. There was no guttering to catch the water from the thatch, and when it rained my Mother used to put a bath on the doorstep to prevent the water running into the house. The doorways were very low, and my Father, who was rather tall, often had a bad bruise on his forehead. In the small bedroom the head of the bed touched one wall and the foot of the bed the other wall. The lean-to roof prevented the bed being pushed far enough sideways to allow the door to open to its full extent. The three oldest boys slept in that room and, as we all had to get into bed at the same side, it was natural for there to be a bit of fun at times — and also some arguments. There was a small window which opened outwards on metal hinges, and we were fond of looking out and watching the owner of the property walking down the path directly beneath us. One morning my older brother dropped an old hair brush on to the bowler hat of the old gentleman, and three days later we found an iron bar had been fixed in the middle of the window frame. After that we felt like caged animals.

There was one paraffin oil lamp which stood on the table near to Mother, who always had plenty of mending to attend to, and the children had to play indoor games, such as 'Ludo', and 'Snakes and Ladders' on the floor in semi-darkness. At regular intervals, according to age, we were informed that it was bedtime. Then the door at the foot of the stairs was opened, for about three minutes, to give a streak of light in the bedroom, and sufficient time to jump into bed.

We were never allowed a lighted candle in case during a mock battle we set fire to something. In fact, the possibility of a fire was never out of the minds of our parents. On one occasion my youngest brother put a bundle of magazines on the fire while my Mother was upstairs, and by the time she was able to get to the fireplace the chimney was well alight. Fortunately my Father saw the smoke from his place of work and was quickly on the scene. He removed the live coals from the grate, and saved the day. This was about eleven o'clock in the morning and as there were no fire engines in those days the soot in the chimney continued to burn well into the afternoon with the possibility of a spark setting fire to the thatched roof. I well remember the very anxious look on my parents' faces as the part of the brick chimney that went through the bedroom was still hot at 10 p.m. As a matter of fact, these three cottages were burnt to the ground in 1919. This was caused by a fire in this same chimney. Fortunately it was noticed in the early afternoon so that all the residents and their belongings were saved. The reader will understand why I've never been attracted to wooden thatched houses. In fact, I would never live in one, under any circumstances.

There was a brick oven built into an out-house, which the tenants of Nos. 2 and 3 were also able to use. This could have caused problems but for the fact that both these tenants were elderly ladies who lived alone, and they were only too pleased to let my mother put her cakes into the oven with their own. The heating and controlling of a brick oven was a work of art, and the setting in during the summer months was a very hot job. But the smell of a freshly baked batch of bread made it all worthwhile.

The good supply of home-baked bread and cakes formed our basic diet, and I am certain was chiefly responsible for the usually good health of all the family. Very often, with the exception of fresh vegetables, there was very little else on the table. Bread and milk were sometimes the menu for breakfast, and it was prepared by pouring boiling water on to a basinful of bread, straining the water off, and covering the bread with skimmed milk and a little brown sugar. There was certainly no danger of a bilious attack. My father kept six hens in the backyard, so occasionally it was boiled eggs for breakfast, although we often had to be content with a half an egg each, accompanied by the threat of having that taken away if we did not stop quarrelling about who had the biggest half. As we lived reasonably near to the school, we were able to get home for our mid-day meal, and my mother always managed to provide a substantial dinner, such as suet dumplings and gravy, beef pudding, and batter and gravy, all with a good supply of vegetables. Sometimes the meal consisted of soup made from three pennyworth of bones, obtained from the butchers shop which was quite near. For a second course we might have jam rolly-poly, spotted-dick, treacle tart, or boiled rice and brown sugar. How my mother contrived to provide three meals a day, every day of the week, is a mystery I have never been able to solve. Feeding a family was only one of the problems that poor people had to contend with. Clothing the children was a constant headache in our family.

New clothes once a year was the usual practice. If the garments were not too badly worn they would be 'handed down' and sometimes friendly neighbours would 'pass on' useful articles of clothing. My mother made good use of her Singer Sewing Machine, and often produced homemade garments, particularly for my sisters. We boys usually had a new suit for the Sunday School Anniversary at the Wesleyan Chapel, and what had been 'Sunday Best' was taken for school and had to last for twelve months. We had two shirts each 'one in the wash, and one out', and after the weekly bath on Saturday, the clean shirt was put on, and it was worn day and night until the next Saturday, unless one was unavoidably caught in a rain storm, when a patched shirt would be found and had to be worn until the regular one was dry. It was probably a good thing that we didn't have a clean shirt for every day, as it would have been a full time job, washing, drying and ironing, and my mother would not have had time to cook the food and we should often have been very hungry.

In common with most families of that period, my parents insisted on good behaviour at the meal table. There was always 'grace' before and after meals, and we never began the meal until my father was in his place, and no one left the table without permission. Bread and butter was usually in ample supply at tea time, but cakes and tarts were luxuries, and were the subject of special requests, my mother keeping a close watch on the numbers so that the stock did not become exhausted before the end of the week. Conversation was limited to one at a time. No elbows were allowed on the table, and the soiling of the table cloth was considered inexcusable. With so many lively youngsters around the table it was always possible that someone should break the rules. When this happened, the offender was gently reminded of his mistake, and if this was not effective a stern warning was issued. If this failed, Father would reach for his hazelnut stick which always stood near the fireplace, and although the stick was seldom used it certainly was a sure deterrent.

Sunday was always accepted as a different day. We were allowed to stay in bed an hour longer, and this gave us a chance to have some very exciting pillow fights. After breakfast those who were old enough were dressed in their Sunday Best, and taken to Sunday School which began at 10 a.m. and finished at 12 noon. Sunday lunch was special, there being a joint of beef on the table, which was served cold with beetroot and pickles, to be followed by apple or rhubarb pie and rice pudding which had been baked in the brick oven. At 2.30 p.m. the older children went with Mother to the Service at the Chapel, while my father took charge of the younger ones, and when weather permitted, pushed the pram along the lane to Halesgrove Cottages where my Grandmother, Hannah Page, lived. After the Service we older boys would join the little family party. Although my parents must have been very tired, they made a practice of taking the family for a walk in the afternoon, or evening, and I have happy memories of those little outings which encouraged me to take an interest in the things of nature. The day ended with the reading of a story by my mother, family prayers, and the passing round of the sweet jar, making it a really special day. Contrary to some people's opinion, Sunday in our house was a happy day and had an influence on our thinking and acting in later life.

Soon after my youngest sister was born in October 1909, we moved into the White Horse Public House, and by that time my eldest brother had obtained a part-time job, for which he was paid one shilling and sixpence a week. This, with the small profit from the business provided my mother with some extra housekeeping money. We now had four bedrooms, and two good living rooms, as well as a kitchen. So we had plenty of room to move around and this was greatly appreciated by all the family. To help cope with the extra work my mother taught myself and my brothers to be useful. As the girls were the youngest in the family they were excused for a few years. One of my jobs was to scrub the tap room floor once a week. As it was a boarded floor and most of the customers wore heavy boots, it was quite hard work, but with a few practical tips from my mother I soon learned how to make a good job of it, for which I received quite a lot of praise, but no wages! Another task that was assigned to me was the washing up of the tea time crockery etc. while my brothers, Ken and Reg were required to do the drying on alternative evenings. As time passed by, Ken formed the idea that he was old enough to do the washing, a suggestion that I firmly rejected, and on one particular evening things came to a head. We argued about it all through the operation, and at the end of it Ken took a mighty swipe at me with the wet tea cloth, which really made my ears tingle. Of course, I was not prepared to accept that without retaliation, so I smartly picked up the bowl of water and gave chase out into the backyard. Once I had got within firing range, I let go and emptied the entire contents over Ken, who was wearing a bright red jersey at the time. So the argument came to an abrupt end, but another problem had been created — how to prevent our parents knowing what had happened. So we had to hang the red jersey on the linen line, and wait for it to dry, before we dare go indoors. Otherwise, both of us would have received a sound thrashing. The White Horse remained the family home for over twenty years, and all of us, apart from my youngest brother, were married before our parents retired and moved into a new house known as 'Restholme', at 1, Ipswich Road.

Chapter 12

LIVING CONDITIONS IN 1913

1913 was the last year of a decade that had seen very little change in village life, so a reminder of living conditions at that time may be of interest to the reader.

General farm workers received thirteen shillings a week, and their working hours were from 6 a.m. to 6 p.m. on five days a week, and 6 a.m. to 5.30 p.m. on Saturdays, with one and a half hours taken out for meals. In the winter time the hours were from 'daylight til dark'. Horsemen and stockmen were paid fifteen shillings, and their hours were from 5 a.m. til 5 p.m., and a one-hour morning and evening on Sunday to feed the horses and cattle. The wages of gardeners and grooms were eighteen shillings a week, for what was termed customary hours, including Sunday work and sometimes overtime. Bricklayers, carpenters etc. usually worked for about four pence an hour. Allowing for a shorter day on Saturday they would be able, if the weather was good, to earn one pound a week. There was no guaranteed week, and building workers were often idle two or three days a week due to bad weather. Shop assistants worked from 8 a.m. to 8 p.m. on three days a week. Wednesdays, from 8 a.m. to 1 p.m., and Fridays and Saturdays from 8 a.m. to 9 p.m. or 9.30 p.m.

A few parents by great effort and sacrifice managed to get their boys apprenticed, and this usually meant going into Ipswich, where the only means of transport was a bicycle. My brother was sent to learn the body building side of the motor industry at Egertons of Northgate Street, Ipswich. The normal hours of work were 6 a.m. to 5.30 p.m., and 1 p.m. on Saturdays, but through the influence of a shareholder who lived in the village my brother was allowed to start work at 7 a.m. He left home at 6.15 a.m. and arrived home at 6.15 in the evening, in all weathers, for about three years. Early in the First World War he joined the Army. Shop assistants had to serve an apprenticeship, and as most shops did not close until after 8 p.m. it meant finding lodgings in Ipswich, and then coming home about 10 p.m. on Saturdays and returning on a bicycle ready for work at 8 a.m. on Monday morning. The amount of wages received was insufficient to pay for their lodgings.

The so-called 'cheap food' of the early 1900's has to be considered in conjunction with the low wages of the period. The price of bread was 2¾d for a 2 lb loaf, but a labourer's wage was only 2½d per hour, while sugar at 3d for 2 lbs was dearer than an hour's labour. Many families had one joint of meat only in a week. Oranges and bananas were only seen at Christmas time. In comparison with wages, clothes were dearer than at the present time. A firm of gent's outfitters in Ipswich advertised their goods with the following slogan, 'Jackson's Shoes and Hats are Fine'. 'Ten and Six, and Three and Nine'. This was more than some men earned in a week.

The famous 'Penny Letter Post' was much more expensive than the present First-Class Post at 16 new pence.

Comparing prices with wages, the 'cost of living' in 1913 was much higher than in 1983. Although several new houses had been built in 1910/11, living accommodation was generally very poor. There was no water supply in any of the cottages, and outdoor pumps and open wells had to be shared by several households. In East Row there was one well for twelve cottages, and it is easy to imagine the difficulties and arguments that arose, particularly on washing days. The residents of these cottages had to share one brick oven, and this again was the cause of many neighbours' rows. Surprisingly, these cottages were the only ones in the village that had a drainage system. At all other properties waste water had to be thrown on to gardens, which in some cases were very small. The lavatory, which was usually a wooden structure, was erected as far from the house as possible, in some cases as much as twenty yards, and it was only a very urgent call of nature that would induce one to pay a visit on a cold winter's night. Paraffin lamps and candles were the only means of lighting. A so called 'reading lamp' stood on the table near to Mother, who made gallant efforts to make and mend clothes for the family, and the children had to amuse themselves with such games as could be played in semi-darkness. Very few households were able to afford a daily newspaper, so the man of the house had no problem about not being able to see to read.

Chapter 13

EMPLOYMENT PROBLEMS

Although farms were not mechanized, there always seemed to be a surplus of labour. There were possibly two reasons for this, the first being that Holbrook was an Open Village, and the second being the common problem of several large families.

Most boys at the age of 13 years went to work on the farms, but few of them intended to stay there. However, the opportunities for other employment were very few. During my school days two young men were accepted into the London Police Force, two others got jobs on the Railways, three emigrated to Canada, and three joined the Army. Joining the Army was considered to be an act of desperation, or evidence of a bad character. One local lad tried to liven things up on the farm where he worked, and on Guy Fawkes day he put a firework on the shaft of a tumbril. The bang frightened the horses and caused them to bolt. The farmer promptly gave him a week's notice. So Dick took the only option open to him — he joined the Army.

It was the early period of the Naval Training Establishment at Shotley, so at the age of 15½ years four boys joined the 'Ganges', where the discipline was very harsh and, although these four lads did not try to escape, many others did. These were lads from many different parts of the country who had no idea of the geography of the area and often made rash attempts to get to a railway station, which, of course, was almost impossible without being detected. The local police were paid a small sum for catching and returning any of these lads to the Ganges. Our police sergeant often made a capture, and would take the boys into his house for a meal and then hire a pony and trap to take them to Shotley. Hence, the villagers knew more about the boys that ran away than they did about the ones who didn't.

In December 1913 I left school and went to work at Red House Farm for Mr Walter Cousins, helping to look after the pigs and cattle. One of my jobs was to keep a watch on the cows for an hour each morning, while they fed on the grass banks around the lanes, eating my breakfast at the same time. It was the custom at that time for farmworkers to start normal hours, that is from six to six on March 1st, but I remember Mr Cousins telling us that Berner's and Wrinch's men were going to leave off at half past five, so we had better do the same. That was the first reduction there had been in the working hours for many years. This was evidence of the dissatisfaction among the workers, although there was no trade union for them.

If conditions were bad for boys they were far worse for girls. It was Domestic Service for them, unless they were fortunate enough to have relatives living in a town or city who could provide a home for them while they found some other form of employment. In most cases the parents were unable to prevent their daughters from going into 'service', and the most they could do was to get them a situation in the best house possible, and the reputation of the family was often a deciding factor. No parent liked the idea of their daughter going into a house where only one maid was kept. Not only was the work likely to be very hard, but it was a very lonely life, as the maid had all her meals in the kitchen alone, and very seldom had anyone to talk to in the evenings. Most girls tried to get into a house where at least three maids were kept, and then, providing the cook or housekeeper was kind and considerate, life was much better than at home. There was good food, fellowship in the servants' hall, and a comfortable bed, so although the training was hard, the maids really enjoyed themselves. Of course, the greatest ambition of parents was to get their daughter into a Mansion or big Hall, the nearest being Woolverstone Hall. Here a large staff was kept, and at one time forty men and maid servants under the supervision of a housekeeper, and a first class butler were employed. One girl, whose parents lived at Markwell's Farm, near to Stutton Church, was accepted as a housemaid at Woolverstone Hall, and on her half days off, walked the four and a half mile journey home, and did the return journey again in the evening, and until she found herself a boyfriend, was accompanied by her father. Providing the girls with the required uniform was very difficult for the parents. It was necessary for each girl to have two dresses, pink or blue, for mornings, and two black ones for afternoons, as well as white aprons, caps and cuffs, and, of course, black stockings. These items, together with her underwear and any other extras that the girl might possess, were neatly packed into a tin trunk, which, in the absence of a lock, was made secure by a strong length of cord. If the place of employment was in the village, the trunk would be placed in a wheelbarrow, which in the evening would be pushed by father with his daughter to her new home. If the 'Big House' was in another village, or in the town, Billie Ling's pony and trap was hired, and the journey made during the day. In either case, this was not a very dignified way to start a new life.

Generally the 'time-off' periods were: first Sunday from 10 a.m. to 1 p.m., second Sunday from 2 p.m. until 9 p.m., third Sunday all day, one day in the week from 2 p.m. until 9 p.m., and once a month one whole day off. Wages varied according to age and experience, etc., with the starting wage as little as ten shillings per month. Most employers gave their maids a fortnight's annual holiday. Many parents were very worried about their girls returning to their place of employment, particularly when it was dark, and so it was usual practice for the father or an older brother to act as escort. Naturally most of the girls strongly resented this and would much rather have been escorted by someone of their own choice, but generally boy-friends and sweethearts were strictly forbidden, and although this attitude on the part of the parents has often been criticised, under the circumstances it was justified.

There was no Health Service, no Sick Pay, and no Unemployment Benefit, so if, for any reason a girl lost her job her parents had to keep her out of an income that was not sufficient to feed and clothe the other members of the family properly. In the case of a girl becoming pregnant, and her parents living in a tied cottage, there was the displeasure of the employer to contend with, and often the parents were told to send the daughter out of the village, which meant sending her to the workhouse. Failing this, the father would be given notice to leave his employment and house. Although by the year 1913 attitudes were changing, there were still some cases where these conditions still prevailed. For families who did not live in tied cottages the above-mentioned problem did not exist, but there was the agonizing question, "Who is going to keep the girl and her baby?" Sometimes the parents of the girl and the boy concerned talked the matter over and persuaded the couple to get married, but this in turn inevitably brought more problems. The alternative was for the girl to go back to Service, and for the child to be brought up by the grandparents, with the mother giving what help she could. Under these circumstances it was not surprising that parents kept a close watch on the movements of their girls, particularly when they first left school.

The parents of boys were just as vigilant. Occasionally there were incidents of a humorous nature, of which I will relate one that was typical of others.

A boy and girl, who lived at Lower Holbrook, were school sweethearts, and made gallant attempts to continue the friendship after they left school, but their little talks together were few and far between. After a few months the girl's parents moved into Otter House, Holbrook, and as the daughter was in service at the 'Branthams' (now known as 'Holbrook Lodge'), it meant walking a mile each way every time she had time off, along the road by the Fish Pond and then up Fir Tree Hill. Bessie had no brothers, so Dad had to be the regular escort. In due course, Dad and the boyfriend, Henry, worked out a plan whereby the duties were shared, and the handover point was at the top of Fir Tree Hill. All this was, of course, unknown to mother. To keep it that way, Dad would sit on the stile for about half an hour and so arrive home at the normal time. But, alas, eventually the news leaked out, and on one certain occasion four lads from Holbrook (myself being one of them) were taking a stroll towards Lower Holbrook when we were overtaken by Bessie's parents. A few minutes later we saw four lads from Lower Holbrook coming to meet us, one of them being Henry, who was suddenly confronted by Bessie's mum brandishing her umbrella in a threatening manner, and in very angry tones said, "Henry Wombell I forbid you to talk or walk with my daughter any more. She's not seventeen yet and I will not have it," and she carried on with this lecture for about five minutes, while Henry listened appearing to be quite unperturbed. After she had decided to resume her journey, Henry exclaimed, "That old woman fared somehow, didn't she. I thought she was going to hit me with that umbrella." After a short while the family moved to another village several miles away, so that finally put an end to Bessie's and Henry's friendship.

However, all boy and girl problems were not settled so easily. One young couple in a neighbouring village were very defiant and eloped to Gretna Green, going through a form of marriage. Fortunately wise parents were able to persuade them to return home, where later they were legally married and lived happily ever after. For myself there was trouble while I was still attending school. The girls in my class were a very nice bunch, but of course there was a special one. She lived at Lower Holbrook and so when I escorted her part of the way home I was invariably late home from school and my mother was quick to discover the reason. I was severely reprimanded and reminded that I hadn't chopped the sticks for the morning fire. The next day I solved that problem by getting the sticks done in the dinner hour. I continued my friendship with May, although the journeys to Lower Holbrook became less frequent and my parents made it quite clear that they did not approve.

In July 1913 a Regatta was held at Holbrook Creek, and, in addition to the water sports, there was a fair with roundabouts, swings, coconut shies, etc. I was fortunate in winning three prizes, which I promptly handed to May, thinking it was the proper thing to do. Of course, news got to my mother and I was given a choice — stop the friendship or she would talk to May's parents. Well 2 to 1 is hard, but 4 to 1 is impossible, so I had to give in. We both left school at the end of the year and May left home and went to live with relatives about forty miles away. I've often thought this might have been part of a concerted plan to stop an undesirable courtship.

Quite recently a small group of people of my generation were talking about our early friendships and the attitudes of our parents to them, and we were all of the opinion that our parents were doing the right thing in being strict, and we also agreed that none of our parents interfered with our choice of partners after we reached the age of 17 or 18 years.

Chapter 14

THE YEAR 1914

It has been said that nothing was the same after 1914. This is obviously a reference to the First World War, but there were signs that changes were about to take place even before the 4th August.

For about two years before that date classes for First Aid Instruction were held in the Working Men's Club by Dr H. P. Sleigh, and these were attended by young women who were being trained as Red Cross Nurses. Some of these trainees were gentleman farmer's daughters, and this in itself was a departure from custom, it being the accepted thing that the daughters of gentry played tennis, arranged flowers, played the piano, and went to parties, but did not enter a profession or train for an occupation. There was a great amount of

The Wedding of Miss Lilian Rodwell to Mr Edmund A. B. Stanley, (H.M.S. Afrida). 3 January 1914.

excitement when one of these ladies, in the person of Miss Lilian Rodwell of the Woodlands, was married to a naval officer, Mr Edmund Alan Stanley on the 3rd January, 1914. Miss Rodwell was one of the Red Cross nurses mentioned above, and other members of the Corps formed a Guard of Honour as the bridal pair left 'All Saints Church'.

There was also evidence that some people were looking for better housing and working conditions, as well as a higher standard of education in the village schools. So, while it was true that the War brought changes, it was also true that it prevented other changes taking place.

A desire for change and better conditions probably prompted me, at the suggestion of my parents, to leave the farm where I had worked for three months and accept a job in Holbrook Flour Mill in April 1914. My wages rose from four shillings to five shillings per week. I left off work at 4 o'clock instead of 5 o'clock on Saturdays, and did not have to go to work on Bank Holidays. There was also the added attraction of working under cover all the year through. Against this was the disadvantage of having to work from 6 a.m. to 6 p.m. in the winter months, whereas on the farm it was from daylight until dark. Another disappointment was the short day hours. A large paper with details of the latest Factory Act was pasted on the wall near to the entrance door to the Mill, and one paragraph stated that 'no person under 17 years of age should work more than 7 hours on one day in the week'. As the day began at 6 a.m., with half an hour taken out for breakfast, one could assume that lads under 17 years would finish work at 1.30 p.m. But what really happened was that a half hour was allowed for dinner, and then we were sent in the summer months to cut the grass on the lawns, and in the winter months had to look after the pigs for two hours. We eventually left off work at the same time as the other workers. That very mean method of avoiding the spirit of the Act caused a 'chip on the shoulder' which I have never been able to get rid of. To add to the injustice the workers were never paid during working hours as the boss never opened the office door until after 4 p.m. By the end of the twelve months I formed the opinion that working in the Mill was no better than working on a farm.

Although there had been a lot of talk about war for many months, it was nonetheless a great shock to everyone when on August 4th Mr Asquith, who was Prime Minister, announced that war had been declared on Germany. Not every household had a daily newspaper, but as the price of the Evening Star was a halfpenny, as against one penny for the East Anglian Daily News, several people had a regular order for 'The Star'. These were brought from Ipswich by Mr John Smith, the local carrier, in his horse-drawn van, and delivered by a local lad on a bicycle. It was the custom at that time for the publishers to send a flysheet with each batch of newspapers, on which was printed the headlines of the day's news. This flysheet was fixed to the front of the deliverer's cycle to help persuade someone to buy the spare copies that he always carried. For the same purpose, the 'Star' boy would shout out the headlines as he did his round. At this particular time, Albert Rush was the 'Star' boy, and as he was coming out of the front entrance to the East Row Cottages, shouting "War declared on Germany", an elderly resident, who was known as 'Dab heel Keeble' was riding his bicycle up the Street towards the Co-op, and although he could ride a bike he certainly couldn't change speed or alter course. Albert intended to cross the road and enter the alleyway beside the Swan Inn, and seeing 'Dab heel' in the centre of the road, decided to go behind him. Unfortunately, the front wheel of his bike just touched the back wheel of Mr Keeble's cycle, and down goes the old gentleman on the road. As he sat there, he said in very stern tones, "Boy, you should be more careful." Albert replied, "I'm very sorry Mr Keeble, but I rang my bell good tightly." This greatly amused some men who were standing nearby, and one of them quickly shouted, "War is declared on Dab heel." Albert was there and then nicknamed 'Tightly', and 'Tightly' he has been ever since, and 'Tightly' he will remain for the rest of his days by those who know him best.

In many ways August 4th, 1914 was the beginning of a new era. Mobilization of the Armed Forces was quickly set in motion. Two young men who were Army reservists were immediately called up, and then a recruiting meeting was held on Church Green, and several young men were enlisted. Others soon responded to the appeal of the Recruiting Officers. No one had any idea what this war would be like; there was talk of three months, and six months, but no one expected it to last for four years. To some lads this was an opportunity to get away from the hum drum of life and the poor working conditions that prevailed at that time. In keeping with other parts of the country, lads were eager to enlist, some of them well under the age of 18 years. My own brother joined the Suffolk Regiment when he was 16 years old, but before he had finished his training my parents informed the War Office of his correct age, and this prevented him being sent Overseas. He was promoted to Corporal, and spent the next two years training recruits at Felixstowe, which at that time was full of soldiers. Most of these belonged to the 3rd Battalion of the Suffolk Regiment, which was the supply for the 1st and 2nd Battalion. One tall and well built lad enlisted when he was 15 years old, and in due course was sent to the battle front. After a few months he was wounded and sent home to England for hospital treatment. His mother then wrote to the War Office, and he was discharged and worked on a farm for twelve months. On his 18th birthday he was recalled to the Colours, and after a short period of re-training was again sent overseas. Before the war ended he was listed as 'Killed in Action', which not surprisingly caused his mother to have a nervous breakdown, from which she never completely recovered.

The fact that this kind of thing happened is an indication of how lads were keen to join up and how anxious the Recruiting Officers were to accept them. The usual practice was for the lad to enter the office and state his correct age, whereupon he would be told by the Officer to go outside and then return saying he was 18 years old. He would be signed on there and then. However, by the end of 1914, when the true nature of the War was beginning to be known, recruitment slowed down considerably and other methods had to be adopted. Firstly, there was an urgent appeal by Lord Kitchener. Posters were put up inviting men to join Kitchener's Army. Later there was the Lord Derby Group Scheme. Men were required to register at the local stations that were set up, and the call up was by age-group, beginning with the youngest. But not everyone registered, and so eventually it was conscription for all men up to the age of 45 years. The reluctance of some men to volunteer can be understood, when one takes into consideration all the facts, as men were coming home on leave and telling terrible stories of what was happening. In the 'East Anglian Daily Times' there were regular long lists of wounded, missing, and killed, of the Regiments closely connected with East Anglia, and married men with children felt they were justified in staying at home as long as possible. Their conscience often troubled them, and they were sometimes subjected to jeers and sneers from people who were certain they would never be called up. One such lady approached Mr Herman Quantrill with the question, "Are you ever going to join the Army?" to which he replied, "I might if there is conscription," but when conscription did come, he joined the Navy and I have often wondered if the lady was very disappointed.

By the end of 1916 the death toll on the battlefield was very high, and every available man was being called up, some of them in grades as low as C.I. There were very few families who did not have someone in the Forces. In some cases three sons were in uniform. One woman, Mrs W. Southgate of Park Cottages was left to care for three younger children whilst her husband and three sons were all in the Army. Fortunately, the husband returned unhurt, but the youngest of the sons was drowned when the troop ship in which he was travelling to the Middle East was torpedoed and sank. The eldest was taken prisoner and was detained in a German Prisoner of War Camp for quite a long period and, just when he was expected home in 1919, a message came through that he had died before being released. The other son was severely wounded while serving with the Royal Artillery, and although he came home, partially disabled, he died a few years later as a result of his War time injuries.

My brother was reported missing on the 28th April, 1917, and in spite of extensive enquiries by the Red Cross and the War Office, he could not be traced, and eventually was listed with those who were 'Presumed to be Dead'.

The men serving overseas were supplied with cards that had printed details on them, such as 'slightly wounded', 'seriously wounded', 'missing', or 'killed in action', and the soldiers were advised to address these to their families, so that in the event of anything happening to them the cards could be forwarded by one of their chums or a member of a hospital staff. Very few days passed without some family receiving one of these cards, and as they were put through the letter boxes there was always the fear that the worst had happened. The list of twenty-four names that appears on the War Memorial is an indication of the suspense and sorrow that was experienced by many families. In addition, a large number of men were discharged as disabled, or suffering from some chronic illness. The pensions granted to these unfortunate men were very small, and in some cases non-existent. In one case a man who had received a serious stomach wound was sent on to a farm to replace an able-bodied man who had been exempted, and after twelve months he had to attend a medical tribunal in connection with his claim for a pension. During that twelve months, due to the kindness of his work mates, he had been able to work continually, and because of this the members of the tribunal disqualified him from being granted a pension. The maximum pension for loss of a limb was twenty-nine shillings per week.

Chapter 15

THE WAR TIME FOOD AND WORK SITUATION

A food shortage was one of the many bad effects of the War, and in contrast to conditions during the Second World War, there was no official rationing, except for meat. The shortage of labour and the large amounts of food needed for the troops were two of the causes of the shortage, but the main cause was the sinking of a large number of food ships by the German submarines. Ships bringing wheat from Canada were among their chief targets, and therefore bread was the first basic food to be in short supply, and that which was available was of a very poor quality.

I was working in Holbrook Flour Mill during 1915 and 1916, and so was acquainted with some of the difficulties that the millers had to contend with. Due to the English climate local grown wheat was very soft, and it was usual to mix with it wheat from Manitoba at the rate of 3 to 1 English. At one time there was very little corn getting through from Canada, so other cereals had to be used, such as White Maize and Beans, and sometimes mouldy wheat had to be added. Much of the flour was of a very poor quality, and housewives were often frustrated, as attempts were made to provide cakes, pastry, and homemade bread for the family. Suet puddings were served up in vegetable dishes, and cakes just fell to pieces. My mother partially solved the problem by mixing potatoes with the flour on a fifty-fifty basis. My father, with my help, cultivated four strips of allotment land, and so we had a good supply of potatoes and other vegetables. Friday was baking day, so on Thursday evenings my three brothers and myself were put on spud bashing duty, and after we had peeled one and a half stones, they were just put into a big pan on an open fire and boiled carefully. My mother made sure they did not go to mash, and after the water was drained off, the pan was stood in front of the fire so the potatoes could dry. Next morning the potatoes were mixed with an equal amount of flour, and then the normal baking procedure commenced. By mid-day a week's supply of wholesome bread was put on the kitchen table to cool, and everyone who tasted these brown crisp loaves agreed they were much better than anything the local bakers could produce.

In the absence of rationing the shop keepers did their best to distribute what food was available. Butter and cheese were always difficult to obtain, and the restricting of each customer to a half pound of each caused a lot of dissatisfaction. A woman with four children could be forgiven for complaining when she knew that a customer with only a husband and herself to keep also received a half pound. Farm workers were greatly helped by the free malt and hops that they were allowed. It was one bushel for the hay harvest and three bushels for the corn harvest. Each bushel would make eighteen gallons of good beer, which incidentally was addictive. This wholesome beverage was consumed in quite large quantities. A man working in the harvest field would probably drink a gallon a day, and it is reasonable to assume that it was a food as well as a drink. The brewing of homemade beer required quite a lot of skill and patience. A copper large enough to hold twenty gallons of water was needed, and two large tubs, which very often had to be borrowed. It took about twenty-four hours to complete the operation, and it required attention late into the night and again early in the morning. Because of this the job was often shared between a man and his wife, although a few women could manage it on their own. Towards the end of the War a Government order made home brewing illegal, except by licence, so the practice was gradually phased out.

Because so many men were in the Forces, farmers and other employers were very glad to employ boys and women, as well as keeping on older workers. In many cases lads of sixteen and seventeen years of age were doing the work of men. I was doing a carter's job at Holbrook Mill when I was sixteen, and received a man's wages for doing it. As a matter of interest, I was never put back on to boy's pay, although after the War a young man had to reach the age of twenty-one years before he received full pay. There were plenty of opportunities to work overtime, so together with cultivating an allotment and looking after two pigs, my time was fully occupied, and this was probably one reason why I did not often get into mischief. I was also able to save about £100, which was all to the good, as it proved to be impossible to save money after the War.

Skilled labour on the farms was very scarce, and the only way a farmer could retain a key worker was to apply for an exemption order from a local tribunal, which consisted of government representatives and a number of local farmers. If an exemption was granted, it was often for three months only, and at the end of that period the man would be 'called up' and a partially disabled man sent to replace him.

By the summer of 1918 the food situation was very serious indeed, and the Government decided that lads of eighteen should not be called up until after the corn harvest. This order applied only to lads working on the farms. As I was eighteen years old on the 12th June I was one of the first boys to benefit from that order. Nevertheless on the 1st June I was given notice to attend the Garnett Hall in Bolton Lane, Ipswich on 14th June for a medical examination. I was passed as 'A.1', in spite of reporting a 'gammy knee'. With the other lads of my age group I was allowed to continue working on the farm until September, and by that time the forces of the Allies were making good progress on the battle fields, and a further Government Order was issued, allowing eighteen year olds to remain on the farms until the root crops were gathered in. By that time the War was nearing its end, and eventually the Armistice was signed on 11th November. So by the 'skin of my teeth' I escaped doing military service.

As a result of the labour shortage, girls were given an alternative to domestic service. They were accepted as shop assistants, and some travelled to Ipswich to work in the factories. So a change took place that was to become permanent.

In 1916 the first daylight saving bill was passed in the House of Commons, and that was a change that both farmers and workers resented. For a few years they insisted on working according to the Old Time, and this added to the difficulties of the housewives. It was hard enough in any case to find sufficient food for three meals a day, but when the time of those meals had to be staggered, it was well nigh impossible. At one time my youngest brother worked at the Co-op Stores, and as the shop did not close for a mid-day meal, his break began at 12.30 p.m. My father's meal time was from 1 p.m. until 2 p.m. Another brother was working at Holbrook Mill and his meal time was from 1.30 p.m. to 2.30 p.m. As I was working on a farm, and my watch was set according to the Old Time, I arrived home for my dinner at 2.15 p.m. Yet another brother, who worked on a farm as a horseman, normally worked until 3 p.m. before going home for dinner. So again, allowing for the difference in the clocks, he arrived for his meal at 4.15 p.m. I often have wondered why my mother did not go crazy.

To encourage food production, a Corn Act was passed which gave the farmers a guaranteed price for their corn. Agricultural Wages Boards were also formed in the counties, as well as nationally. The farmers had four representatives on these boards. The Workers' Union had four, and there were three independent members appointed by the Government. Applications for wage increases were made by the Workers' Union to the County Boards, and when a decision was reached a recommendation was forwarded to the National Board. Later a paper would be published stating the new wage rate, which varied slightly from one county to another. The net result of this procedure was that the wages of farm workers rose from thirteen shillings in 1914 to forty-five shillings in 1919 for a fifty-seven hour week, with nine shillings extra for stockmen and horsemen. Strenuous efforts were made from time to time for a reduction in the number of working hours, and in 1918 it was agreed by the National Wages Board that the minimum number of working hours should be fifty-four per week. This caused great rejoicing among the workers, who for the first time could look forward to Saturday afternoons off, but hope was turned to dismay when the farmers ordered that work should begin at 6.30 a.m. instead of 6 a.m., thus absorbing the three hour reduction order by the Board. This was a typical example of keeping the letter of the law and ignoring the spirit of it, but by 1920 there was a further reduction in the working hours, and then the principle of a 'Saturday Half-Day' was accepted by the farmers.

Chapter 16

ROAD CONDITIONS

The basic materials for road surfaces were stones picked from the fields, and granite stones brought in by barge to Holbrook Creek, and in spite of constant attention by the local roadman, many loose stones were to be seen, especially after a flock of sheep had been driven from one farm to another. One of the local postmen, who cycled to Bentley Station and back six days a week, considered himself fortunate if his cycle tyres were not punctured more than once a week.

The road from Ipswich to Shotley was very badly affected by the heavy solid tyred lorries that were used to convey large coils of thick wire needed in the manufacture of submarine protection nets. At one time chalked covered flint stones were put on to the road in an effort to prevent the road being completely churned up, but in a few months the stones had disappeared, and all that could be seen were huge pools of chalky slush.

The stretch of road between the bottom of Freston Hill and Ipswich was in a very bad condition, due partly to the river water coming on to the road. This happened quite often as the road in many places was much lower than at the present time. There was a good footpath on top of the bank, beside the road, and it was a common sight to see cyclists pushing their bicycles along this path, as the water was too deep to ride through. Of course, horses could get through without any difficulty, so no one was greatly alarmed when there was a high tide. After the end of the War the road was made about eighteen inches higher, and since then has not been flooded so frequently, and never to the same extent.

One incident that comes to my mind was typical of many others; a workmate and myself decided to go into Ipswich one Saturday evening to do a little shopping. On the return journey it was necessary to light the lamps on our cycles, one at the front and one at the back of each machine. These were oil burning lamps as the light from Acetylene lamps would have been too bright. As we came over Bourne Bridge we overtook two people who were walking, and we had so much trouble keeping our lamps alight that the walkers got to the Red House Cottages first! There and then we both vowed that we would not cycle to Ipswich again until the War was over and the roads repaired.

The bad state of the roads was also evident when visits were made to the men who were stationed in Felixstowe. It was almost impossible for parents or wives to visit the soldiers and so younger brothers often volunteered to undertake the journey, during the summer months but never during the winter. It was the usual practice for a small group to travel together, probably once a month.

The chief reason for this was to help each other if there was cycle trouble, particularly punctures. It was very hard work, and each journey took about two hours to complete, and the one or two houses where soft drinks were available were well patronized. Thinking about those times, it seems incredible that men stationed so near to their homes should be so isolated from their families. Their periods of leave were few and far between. In most cases it was two or four days leave, during a training period of about thirteen weeks, and these few days were mostly spent working in the garden so that their families might have some vegetables to eat during the coming winter.

Chapter 17

THE LIGHTER SIDE OF WARTIME LIFE

Although life in general was hard and grim there were times of humour and laughter which helped to brighten the days of fear, hardship and sorrow.

On the farms there were always one or two men who could cause a bit of fun, sometimes at the misfortune of a fellow worker. On the farm at which I worked there was a certain horseman, 'Jim', who had never learned how to control his horses properly and quite often while Jim was attaching one horse to the implement he intended to use the other horse would very quietly move a few yards away, and if he was not noticed would soon start walking back to the stable. If Jim tried to stop him by running, the horse would break into a trot, and was soon back at the stable. As the fields were big, and the hedges low, this episode could be seen a long way off, and the cry would go round the farm, "Old Jolly has done it agin," and for the next few days Jim had to endure quite a lot of good-humoured teasing.

Other incidents, such as ploughing that was not straight and stacks that were not upright and unpunctuality for work were all opportunities for friendly jeering, which everyone had to accept at some time or another.

The evening meeting place for most of the lads was the Reading Room where we were able to forget work and the War, and take part in indoor games, such as draughts, rubber quoits, billiards etc. Not surprisingly a few harmless pranks were indulged in, such as tying the Committee man's jacket to the back of his chair, putting the paraffin lamp out, and leaving him to free himself in the dark. Of course, this did not happen very often. There were six committee men, who each did duty on one evening each week, and naturally there were only certain men who were given the above treatment. The man on duty was not always there when the doors opened, and on one such occasion there were just six of us present, and the four youngest began to kick a football around the floor, something that was strictly forbidden. As I, at 18 years of age, was the eldest of the group, I warned the lads about this, but they all promised that they would be very careful, so I settled down to reading the newspaper. Eventually the expected happened, and a large pane of window glass was broken, and that quickly put a stop to footballing. In the silence that followed I pointed out to them that they must inform the secretary before someone else did. They took my advice and offered to pay for the damage. When the bill was given to them I was at home suffering from a mild attack of 'flu, and the youngest boy came to the house and asked my mother if he could speak to me. He was shown into the room where I was, and quickly came to the point with the following demand, "Pedlar, I want eighteen pence out of you." To which I replied, "What for?" "To help pay for the broken window," he explained. "But I wasn't playing with the football," I protested. "That makes no difference," he retorted, "you were there, so you were just as bad as the other lads." I very willingly paid up, and Sydney, who was 15 years old, left the room with a saucy grin on his face, and made his way to the secretary's house. So the debt was paid and we were set free. We were a high-spirited, mischievious bunch of lads, but we accepted an unwritten code of conduct which included making good any damage done to other people's property or possessions.

In the summer months the Reading Room was very useful as a meeting place, although few indoor games were played. Tales would be told of anything of interest that had happened during the day, and often a good bit of horseplay was indulged in. Then a challenge thrown out for a walking or running race round the village would be quickly accepted, and the rest of the evening would be devoted to such simple pastimes, with no prizes offered.

As most of the lads worked from 6 a.m. til 5.30 p.m. they were ready for bed by 10 p.m. and were not likely to cause disturbing noises late into the night. As the pubs closed at 10 p.m. it was very unusual for anyone to be walking through the village after 10.15 p.m. The only exceptions were the light summer evenings when the Zeppelins were expected and we gathered at the Post Office corner to listen and watch. The Police Sergeant who was in charge of the area lived next door to the Post Office where the only telephone in the village was installed, and messages were received in morse and passed on to the Police Officer. Another indication that Zeppelins were over the North Sea was the restlessness of pheasants, and when this happened the gamekeeper would hurry to the corner and very excitedly declare that he was sure "They were on the way." We lads were much more interested in his state of nervousness than we were in the possibility of an Air Raid. As might be expected, the Policeman often resented our presence, and after several attempts to quieten us, would at about 11 p.m. give us our marching orders, saying it was time young boys like us were in bed. As our parents were of the same opinion we very reluctantly went home leaving a few men on watch.

There was a very tall telegraph post near to the Post Office, with metal brackets fixed to enable the linesmen to carry out repairs. One evening George Marjoram managed to climb to the top of the post, to the great delight of the rest of the gang who were very anxious to know if he could see anything. Very soon George was spotted by Sergeant Charles Smith, for that was the Policeman's name, (although we had nicknamed him 'Pickles') who very sternly ordered him down, and by way of punishment gave all of us our 'marching orders'.

On another occasion, a man who was in the habit of doing unusual things after drinking about three pints of beer, pretended to be an army corporal, and formed a group of us into a squad and proceeded to drill us in preparation for our call-up. Needless to say, this did not meet with the approval of the Police Sergeant, and he soon gave us our marching orders for home, and reprimanded Jimmie for being such an old fool.

It has always been a mystery to me as to why some people plainly invited youngsters to play pranks on them. Such a couple lived at Roslyn House in The Street, not far from the Reading Room. If things got very quiet there was always Nancy Lemon and her daughter, Ethel, to stir up. Someone would suggest going for a walk, and we then proceeded down the street cracking jokes and laughing loudly. When opposite the house, the lad on the pathway would touch the latch of the iron gate, which thereupon opened of its own accord, and in a moment the bedroom window was thrown open and Nancy's head appeared. At the same time the door opened and Ethel rushed into the road uttering all the threats and warnings she could think of. According to a pre-arranged plan we continued walking and talking while Ethel carried on with her threats, as she walked backwards in front of us until she became exhausted and gave it up as a bad job. During the next few evenings we would walk past without touching the latch, and then after about ten days the performance would be repeated, to the great delight of the neighbours. Ethel and Mother must have wasted many hours waiting for the click!

The presence of wounded soldiers in the area made life a little more interesting for the village girls, some of whom were now working in munition factories and shops, and therefore had their evenings and Sundays free of duties. The nearest convalescent home was at Woolverstone House, so small groups of girls, some walking, some on bicycles, regularly made their way to the village of Woolverstone. Here they would meet rivals from other villages who were not always friendly, and when little skirmishes took place the soldiers thought it was great fun. A few serious friendships were formed, but as the soldiers' stays were mostly short ones, the couples were soon parted, and I never heard of a marriage resulting from these friendships.

It may seem strange that the memory of a funeral should cause anyone to smile, but I think anyone would be without a sense of humour if they could not see something funny in the following story; the man who hired the Woodlands Farm, Charles Smith — better known as 'Swanky', died in October 1914, and great interest was created in the village when it was known that he had directed that the coffin should be taken to the Church in one of his farm waggons. So on the fixed day, the horseman washed the best waggon, polished the harness of Ruby the fine black mare, and arrived at the front gate at the appointed time. The local undertaker, Mr Henry Rogers, was there with the bearers who were all local men, and after ascertaining that the mourners were ready, supervised the moving of the coffin into the front hall. Then there was a hitch in the proceedings! It was the custom in those days to give the bearers a glass of home-brewed beer as soon as they entered the house, but it so happened that although there was a large family, four sons and five daughters as well as the widow, no-one thought of the 'home-brewed' until the coffin was placed in the hall. But acting on the principle that it's 'Better late than never', the beer was duly brought, poured into glasses which were placed on the coffin, and the bearers, two on either side of the coffin, drank to the memory of dear old Swanky, much to the disgust of the undertaker. As the old gentleman had been a very heavy beer drinker, everyone in the village was sure that he was highly delighted that the men were not done out of their ration.

So for Holbrook, 1914 was indeed a memorable year, with a Society Wedding in January, War declared in August, and a very unusual funeral in October.

CHAPTER 18

THE AFTERMATH OF WAR

During the winter of 1918-19 there was a very bad epidemic of influenza which probably began in the War Zones and spread throughout the British Isles, and even reached Canada where an uncle of mine died as a result of it. I have been told by older people that it was the first outbreak for more than thirty years, and it caught the medical profession unprepared, being quite unable to cope with the very unusual number of patients. One lad who worked for Dr. Carey at The Beeches, jokingly told his chums that he mixed up pink medicine in a tub each morning, and the doctor gave everyone who came to the Surgery a bottleful of this mixture whether they had 'flu or not. Teenagers and people in their early twenties were very badly affected, and the fever developed so quickly that often the patients were unable to get home from their place of work, particularly those who worked in factories. I personally went to work one morning feeling quite well, but by 11 o'clock I was too ill to continue and had great difficulty in getting home. My mother helped me into bed, where I stayed for three days, with a very high temperature. It was useless to send for the doctor, so I just sweated it out, and received what nursing my mother could give me. She must have done the right things, as I was out and about as soon as my chums who had been given medicine by the doctor. The convalescent period was about ten days and we met in groups and spent most of the time relating our own individual experiences which were often quite funny; one lad said when he first got out of bed the floor wasn't there!!

Probably as a result of the War two Acts of Parliament were passed in 1918. The first gave the right to vote to all men of 21 years, and to women of 30 years, which doubled the electorate to twenty millions. This gave most of the men who served in the War an opportunity to have a say in how the country should be run, and many of them had strong views about that, and expressed them at the next election. There had been quite a lot of talk of making Britain, "A Country fit for heroes to live in", but when some of the men discovered that they had no jobs to go to and no unemployment benefit, they became very angry and bitter. Those who unfortunately had been wounded, or had contracted some incurable disease were treated very badly, and this led to quite a lot of ill-feeling in the village. At a Parish meeting held in March 1919 a very heated debate took place on the question of the nature of a War Memorial. In a schoolroom crowded with parishioners, many of whom were not on the electoral roll, many hard things were said, and after it was eventually decided to erect a stone memorial on the Church Green there was a bitter argument about the suggested wording. Some people strongly criticized the phrase "They *gave* their lives for their country", contending that the victims of the War were driven to their death. This unfortunate division of opinion was a reflection of the general feeling in the village.

The second Act of Parliament raised the school leaving age to 14 years, and this helped to reduce the number of people unemployed, but it did not prevent the number rising to one million in 1922. Unemployment was only one of the problems that had to be faced, as the men continued to be released from the Forces. There were difficulties for some at home. Children of three to five years had grown up without knowing their fathers, and some men found it very difficult to take their rightful place in the family, and the older children often resented being disciplined by their father. In some cases gardens had been neglected, and in spite of much hard work, failed to produce sufficient vegetables for the family's needs, and this caused friction between man and wife.

There were problems too for the single men. Wartime experiences had changed the views and characters of some. In some cases there was no desire to settle down in their home village. Some had met new girlfriends in other parts of the country. The girls too had often changed and had no wish to resume old courtships, and while there were some humourous stories to be told there were also some genuine heartaches.

In the home there were difficulties that had to be faced. Younger brothers and sisters had grown up, which caused the small cottages to be overcrowded, and it was possible that the returning serviceman would feel that he wasn't wanted, and that made it very hard for the parents.

For those who renewed old friendships and were anxious to get married, there was the problem of finding somewhere to live. There just were not any houses available. Because of the acute shortage of living accommodation the District Council decided to build some houses for letting. Some of the first of these were six semi-detached houses in Ipswich Road. Although it was estimated that ten million young men were killed in the War, and a greater number than that died from diseases, there was a surplus of labour by the time the last of the servicemen were demobbed. It was a great relief to know that the fighting had stopped when the Armistice was signed. However, the suffering and hardship continued, and in some cases increased.

Britain had lent vast sums of money to the Allies, and by the time the War ended we owed the United States of America nine hundred and twenty million pounds. This situation caused drastic measures to be taken by the government, one of which was the repealing of the Corn Act, which provided for a guaranteed price to farmers for their corn. This caused a sharp drop in the price of cereals and the farmers suffered a great loss. Inevitably this affected wages and by 1922 farm workers' minimum wages had dropped from forty-five shillings to twenty-five shillings per week. In addition, the Agricultural Wages Board made a ruling that no one under twenty-one years of age should receive full wages. As some of the ex-servicemen were still under the required age, there was a great deal of resentment and bitterness, and there was great dissatisfaction among those who had received full wages for more than two years and now had to take a reduction of two shillings per week. Very soon tenant farmers became bankrupt and land owners were unable to find new tenants, so many acres of land were put down to grass of left derelict. Labour conditions were also very bad in the nearby town of Ipswich, and men were coming into the villages in search of work. Although, as I have already mentioned, prices of food etc. were lower than during the War, they had not fallen by the same proportion as wages, and many people were really desperate. As time went on conditions got worse instead of better, and so began the period known as the Great Depression.

Although it had no connection with the War, the burning to the ground in 1920 of three thatched cottages that stood where the present petrol filling station is situated, added to the feeling of depression which was present in the village. Coupled with the thankfulness that no lives had been lost, and little damage done to furniture, there was sadness at the realization that there were three fewer homes in the village. This sadness was increased by the fact that the occupants of one of the cottages had just lost a member of the family who had died while serving in the Royal Navy, and his remains were to be buried in Holbrook Churchyard the next day.

Chapter 19

LIVING CONDITIONS DURING THE GREAT DEPRESSION

It was inevitable that as conditions got worse the parents of young children should face the greatest problems and their families suffer from malnutrition. Some employers did their best to help by employing married men in preference to single chaps, and the local authorities paid part rent subsidies to the tune of one hundred million pounds. There was no unemployment benefit for farm workers and often an unemployed single man had to be kept by his parents or brothers.

The District Council provided work for a few men on a road-widening scheme between Holbrook and Freston crossroads, but unfortunately this was never completed. The national unemployment figure was one million in 1922, and rose to one million and two hundred thousand by 1929. The majority of people were not having

Cutting corn on site of Royal Hospital School. 1928.
(W. Scott and W. Page).

sufficient food, and there was quite a lot of illness, particularly among young people. In one family four daughters died of T.B. in five years.

By 1926 the brick works had closed for good, and the owner of the flour mill had become bankrupt so that business was also closed down, putting several more men on the unemployment list. In contrast to present conditions, mechanization was not responsible for the vast number of workless men, as the only machines to be seen on the farms were self-binders for harvesting the corn, and threshing machines, and as very few married women were working the trouble could not be attributed to them. The first Fordson Tractor to come into the Shotley peninsula was put to work on the site of the Royal Hospital School in September 1926, and the writer was the driver. The back wheels were fitted with iron streaks and the front wheels had a three inch rib to prevent side slip. The spark came from the flywheel through a distributor, (the roller of which ran in oil) to the coil boxes and then to the sparking plug. Self-starters were unknown then, and the starting of the engine particularly in damp weather was indeed a major operation, and sometimes an unsuccessful one, when after about an hour's cranking nothing was produced but large drops of sweat. The cover would be replaced, and the tractor left until the next morning, when probably the engine would be started in about ten minutes.

During the period from 1919 to 1926 living conditions consistently worsened, and there was a general atmosphere of frustration and depression, particularly among the young people who were in their early twenties. War conditions had prevented the young men from entering an apprenticeship, and so, without a trade, they were doomed to be unskilled workers for the rest of their lives, and to many there was no hope of work of any description. For those who were at work there was very little to be cheerful about, as there were no prospects of getting a better job or higher wages.

The consideration of marriage added to the feeling of disappointment. Many young women were tired of the drudgery of domestic service, and desired to have a home of their own. The young men were very conscious of the fact that they could not provide the kind of home that they both desired and deserved, and this caused a great deal of frustration. A few of the girls decided to look for someone who was receiving a higher wage, and therefore broke off the engagement and found employment in London where the wages were higher. Some young couples resigned themselves to the conditions, and decided to get married as soon as a cottage was available, and to be content with the minimum of furniture etc. until such time as they would be able to acquire enough additional items to make what could be termed a comfortable home. Some of the boys took a different attitude and decided to postpone any idea of marriage to a future time, which in some cases never came. I myself decided to take the plunge when I was 26 years old, after much serious thought and consideration with my sweetheart, who in common with other girls was tired of domestic service. As a result of doing a man's job during the day, as well as cultivating an allotment, and keeping one or two pigs, I had managed to save about one hundred pounds. This we estimated would buy the essentials for a home, but for about a year we looked without success for a small cottage, and in addition we had to face the very real possibility that I might become unemployed. For my parents' sake, as well as our own, we both realized that we should have our own home, because with three brothers as well as myself, my mother was certainly overworked.

The general atmosphere of depression that prevailed, and my own problems had had a bad effect on me, and by this time I was on the verge of a nervous breakdown. I realized that I had to do something to prevent this condition getting worse so when I was offered a job driving a tractor on a farm and a tied cottage to live in, I gladly accepted and we were married on 9th October, 1926. By agreeing to do some Sunday work and a little overtime, I earned £2 per week, but after rent, coal and insurances were paid my wife had only 27 shillings for house keeping. However, we were quite happy as many people had much less than that to live on. At that time I was secretary of the Holbrook Rovers Football Club, and played regularly in the Ipswich District League Matches, and although I regretted doing so, I decided that I must give up football altogether, and devote my spare time to running a home. Naturally I received a bit of jeering from some of my chums, with such comments as, "I can see that you are under petticoat government," or, "I suppose you're afraid to leave the Missus," but I knew that they understood what the real reason was.

The hours of work were from 6.30 a.m. to 5.00 p.m., Monday till Friday, and 6.30 a.m. to 1.00 p.m. on Saturday. In the summertime there was often a few hours' overtime to be worked. I had a

Holbrook Steel Quoit Club. 1927.
Back row left to right — Bob Driver, Ken Page, Jack Thurston, Bert Stannard, Bill Curtis, Jim Knights.
Middle row — Albert Rush, Bill Smith, Charles Dunnett, Rev. Brent Neville, Bert Dunnett, Ted Hughes.
Front row — Wally Driver, Reg Page.

large garden, and like most men I grew as many vegetables as possible, because, "what you didn't grow you didn't have". There was no money available for buying vegetables, and in the winter months there was fire wood to be carted and cut in order to save coal. When our first child was born, I felt it was my duty to be nursemaid on a Saturday afternoon so that my wife could go up to the village for an hour or two — so the reader will understand that I simply did **not** have time to play football. While I was very busy providing for my wife and child, and later on four children, some of my pals were idling their time away and becoming more and more depressed. The situation became so bad that they didn't expect to find work. During the summer of 1927, two of them, Bob Simpson and Ernie Ling, went regularly down to Holbrook Creek, taking a bottle of cold water with them. They lay on the grass until high tide, had a swim, and then sat on the grass till the evening when they returned home to a very meagre meal. Their mothers were widows, and as Bob and Ernie were not receiving Unemployment Benefit it must have been a terrible experience for all of them.

A ray of hope came to the area when work began on the Royal Hospital School in 1928. The contractors, Gerard & Sons gave work to several local skilled and unskilled men, but there were so many unemployed that the firm could not absorb them all. Many men walked from Ipswich and other places each morning hoping to get set on, and it was pathetic to see the look of disappointment on their faces as so many of them were turned away and told to come again the next morning. The situation got so bad that some men resorted to bribery in an effort to get a job, and it was common knowledge that some of the gangers had more free beer than they could drink whenever they went into a Public House. It was certainly not all roses for the men who were fortunate enough to get on to the payroll; most of the work was hard manual labour, and for those who had been unemployed for a long period it was impossible to keep up with the pace that the gangers set. In spite of working very hard for two hours or more, a two minute rest could be the cause of instant dismissal, with the result that on some days there were more men leaving the site than were coming on to it. The brick rubble that was used for road making was brought into Holbrook Creek by sailing barges which were piloted in by Mr Hermon Quantrill. The rubble was then transferred to lorries, and this was particularly hard work, done with bare hands or shovels, and several men collapsed and had to leave the job. So while there was a feeling of relief and thanksgiving that so many men had found employment in the building of the School's extensive premises, there was much criticism of the contractors for adopting what could rightly be described as slave labour methods to get work done. On the credit side, as the result of one of the directors keen interest in the National Children's Home, several of their boys were apprenticed to various trades and must have been a great help to them in future years. The contractors arranged for lodgings in the village for these boys, who evidently appreciated all that was done for them by the people with whom they were billeted. They also soon became friendly with the other young people of the village, particularly the girls. In fact, the friendships were so good that at least three of the lads married local girls, and as far as I am aware "lived happily ever after". For those people who have no knowledge of the building of the School, it may be impossible to visualise the site as it was before 1928. Instead of terraces there was a gradual slope from the main road to the marshes with a clear view of the river and creek. The whole area was cultivated by the family firm of farmers, W. Wrinch & Sons, and consistently produced first-class crops of various kinds. These farmers owned sailing barges that travelled to and fro between Harwich and London. Hay, straw, and Mangold Beet were taken to London for the horses and cows, and the 'muck' from the stables and cowsheds were brought back to be ploughed into the land. As transport became mechanized and fewer horses were kept in London, the barges were often loaded with warehouse refuse and street sweepings, and the unloading of these freights was a very unpleasant operation. There was a quay, known as the 'New Found Out', near to Markwells Farm, where the barges were loaded and unloaded. Because the water was shallow in this small creek the barges could only get in on a very high tide which usually occurred around mid-day or midnight. If the barge arrived at mid-day the crew would take the hatches off, and release some of the foul smell, but if it came in on the night tide they did not have time to do this, so when the farm hands opened up to begin unloading they got the full force of what was known as the 'London Perfume'. If it was light, unloading began at 5 a.m. with six men in the 'hold' throwing the muck on to the deck and five men loading it into 'tumbrils' (Farm Carts). Very often the cargo had become heated on the journey, and the steam that rose from it was thicker than a November fog. At the end of two hours' hard work a break was taken for a drink and a snack, and in spite of the steam and stench everyone would tuck in to what some people would call a substantial meal. There were no facilities for the washing of hands, and if there was a newcomer in the gang who was not accustomed to these very primitive conditions, he probably would not be able to even think of eating food, but if he did not eat he would certainly be a casualty before the end of the day. The work was so hard that no one could survive eight hours of it without plenty of food and drink, and by the time the last cart load left the quay everyone was well and truly tired out. The loading of a barge with straw and hay was a very skilful job. A stack had to be built on the deck with the outside layer overhanging two sides of the barge, and the bales had to be stacked in such a manner that the centre bales could be removed to allow room for the mast to be lowered before going under the bridges in the Thames. There were three of these between Tower Bridge and the wharf where the barge would be unloaded, so that involved lowering and raising the mast three times, and as there were usually only two men on board, it must have been a very arduous task. The alternative was to hire a tug, but as this had to be paid for out of the crew's voyage money, most men preferred to do it the hard way. The voyage to London could be very unpleasant, and sometimes dangerous as the steering wheel was at the rear and the skipper was unable to see the way ahead. Hence the mate had to stand on top of the stack and shout information down to the skipper. It certainly was not a fit job for a semi-invalid.

As the building of the Royal Hospital School neared completion, it was evident that the numbers of unemployed in the area would be increased. A few men obtained employment in the Maintenance Department or on the Ground Staff, but a large number of the contractors' employees had to go on the dole. At one time there were so many men out of work that the Ministry of Labour decided to open an office at Holbrook Post Office, and every morning several people lined up to sign on. One man tried to console a newcomer to the ranks with the suggestion that the first three months were the worst. There was a rise in farmworkers' wages of 8% between the year 1924 and 1929, and later they were given 3 days' annual holiday, but in the main one year was little different from another. So time passed from the 1920's to the 1930's without there being any evidence that better times were coming.

Unusual events in the village during the period of the General Depression added to the gloom and atmosphere of hopelessness. I am reminded of the tragic death of one of my cousins who was in his early twenties, when he fell from a Walnut tree and broke his neck. Before his family recovered from this terrible shock, an uncle of the young man fell from his bicycle and died from a similar injury. In the space of ten years three family doctors died at comparatively early ages, and following short illnesses. The first sad surprise came with the death of Dr J. T. Titterton in August 1927, at the age of 55. Less than three years later Dr H. P. Sleigh died of Pneumonia at the age of 55 years, and then in March 1937 Dr A. H. Andrew died, unexpectedly, at the age of 53. There was also the case of a young man who was killed in a motor cycle accident, and that of a young wife who died in child birth, as well as that of a middle-aged man who died of pneumonia and left a widow and five young children. Even the opening of the Royal Hospital School led to more sadness and sorrow, as news spread of several sudden deaths, and at least one case of suicide among the resident staff during its early days. There was a rumour circulating that an Indian Witch had put a curse on the previous owner and his money, and now many people were inclined to believe that the curse was in operation.

Chapter 20

METHODS AND CONDITIONS OF FARMING

The part of the Holbrook House Estate which included two sets of premises, namely 'The New Buildings' and 'Markwells' was farmed in very much the same way as other farms in the district. There were twelve working horses, a few colts, about forty head of cattle, and sometimes a flock of sheep. The crops grown included wheat, oats, barley, clover, and root crops for cattle feed, and as the land was 'in good heart' some very heavy crops were produced. All the cultivation was done by horse power, and it was a pleasant sight to watch six pairs of horses guided by six good ploughmen who were all intent on drawing a straight furrow.

The methods of controlling horses varied, and although reins were always used, much of the control was done by word of mouth, or to be more precise by peculiar noises. 'Click, click' was the signal to move. 'Gee-Up' meant go a little faster. 'Cup-wee' was change of direction to the left, and 'Grr Werday' to the right, while 'Whoa-there' was the command to stop. Individual horsemen often had additional noises and calls, some of which ought not to be put into print. Horses have a very keen sense of smell, and some men took advantage of this. A horse would become very friendly with a man whose clothes had been sprinkled with certain sweet smelling drugs. On the other hand, it would not move if something very unpleasant had been sprinkled on the ground in front of it. It has often been said that horses' ears are more sensitive than man's, and I think it is true because I have known a horse to respond to an order given in a whisper, when it was at least ten yards from its master, and yet surprisingly some men persisted in shouting very loudly to their team. One such man was George Powell, who lived at 'Markwells', and very often the peacefulness of a lovely summer morning would be shattered by 'Moggy', 'Captain', 'Git up there' or 'I'll Welt yer', and his mates who might be working about a quarter of a mile away would smile and say, "Hello, Powell is about."

In the autumn and spring there was much activity on the fields, as the drilling of corn took place, wheat in the autumn and oats and barley in the spring. The horses were mostly put to work in teams of three, two teams drawing the heavy harrows that broke the soil down into a fine tilth, and the third team drawing the coulter drill which inserted the seed to a depth of three to four inches, and a pair of horses would draw a set of light harrows which were used to ensure that all the seed was covered. The drilling of corn was a very important job, and the farmer was anxious about three things. Firstly, the seed must be put in at the right depth, secondly the 'ringes' (rows) should be straight, and thirdly, he wanted ten acres drilled each day. To encourage the drillmen to do this he paid them a halfpenny each per acre, which was greatly appreciated by the men, and often proved to be a good investment by the farmer. The drill-men knew that if they did not do the job satisfactorily, they would lose it and with it their little extra cash. So they made strenuous efforts to keep in the farmer's 'Good Books'.

Probably the busiest time of the year was the corn harvest in which every workman was involved and also many of the women and children. Although changes had taken place during the War it was still a fact that the sooner the corn was all in the sooner the workmen got their money. Before the War there was a system operating which was known as 'Taking the Harvest'. This was, in fact, a contract between the farmer and the workmen, when agreement was reached between them that the corn would be cut, 'shocked', and stacked for a certain sum. There were slight variations from one farm to another, but the usual figure was seven pounds, with an extra shilling for leather gloves, and another shilling that was known as 'binding money' which was the equivalent of signing a contract. There was also an allowance of three bushels of malt and three pounds of hops per man, with smaller amounts for younger workers, and the home-brewed beer made from these was the main beverage of the harvester. The men who were unable to get home for their midday meal took four or six pints of homebrewed in a stone bottle each morning, and were very careful to keep these well protected from the sun. They therefore had a supply of pleasant drink throughout the day.

During the War years the custom of contracting for the harvest was abolished, probably due to the shortage of able-bodied men, and the newly-formed wages board arranged for the extra hours that had to be worked. These were paid for by a bonus, the amount of which was from four to five pounds per man. This system was not very satisfactory, as no account was taken of the number of acres that had to be harvested, or the conditions of the crops, so that on some farms men were working far many more hours than was reasonable.

Later on another change took place which was against the workers' interest when the Government of the day decided that a licence was necessary for the making of home-brewed beer. As few men were prepared to pay the licence fee, the farmers took the opportunity of stopping the malt allowance without making a cash adjustment to compensate the workers. Without their favourite beverage the harvesters became more dependent on other drinks, so the womenfolk arranged for bottles of hot tea to be taken into the fields two or three times a day. This duty was mostly performed by children who usually received a few coppers as payment.

This brief and incomplete account of harvest customs gives an indication of what village life was like during the month of August. The gathering in of the corn was the first priority, and almost everyone had some share in it. No social events were held, and there were no week night meetings at the Church or Chapel. For the men it was work, eat, and sleep, and for the womenfolk it was a continuous round of preparing meals, keeping the children under control, and mending clothes.

I would like to mention one thing of interest about the eastern side of Holbrook Creek. At the point where the footpath from the Hermitage comes on to the little beach there was at one time a coal house. In 1926 an old gentleman by the name of Thomas Lait informed me that when he first married he lived in the cottage that adjoined the coal shed, and that his wife had the duty of weighing out coal to the customers who came from the villages round about with pony carts to purchase fuel for their use. Mr Lait was 90 years old when he related this so I estimate that he and his wife lived there in about the year 1860. The business was run by a Mr Cornell, who also owned Holbrook Flour Mill, and the coal was brought into the small creek by sailing barges. Perhaps some of my readers could inform me of the date of the closure of this business.

Chapter 21

FAMILY LIFE IN THE 1930s

By the time our second daughter arrived in 1931, my wife was finding it more and more difficult to make the housekeeping money go round, and I was anxiously looking for an opportunity to get a job with a higher wage. However, as I lived in a tied cottage there was very little prospect of that happening, because I not only needed a better job, I also needed a house to live in, and so it was a case of just 'plodding on', trying to keep cheerful. I had always been strongly opposed to the tied house system, and now I was firmly convinced that it was the cause of a great deal of injustice and hardship, but I could not see a way of escape. A change of management at the farm eventually made things more difficult, as different methods of cultivation were used, and fewer men employed to do the work. By 1935 our family had increased to three girls and one boy, and the feeding and clothing of them was well nigh impossible. We were therefore grateful for the help that we received from relatives and friends. I think the most frustrating aspect about our family life was the fact that we could not afford to take the children out for a day's trip, even when I was given three days annual holiday. Of course, our experience was not very different from that of many other families, and it seemed that there was very little that could be done about it. The farmers were still getting only a very low price for their produce, so it was useless for the Trade Unions to press for higher wages. Before the 1914-18 War it was considered possible for a farmer to make a profit if the price of a sack of wheat was the same as a man's weekly wage, but in the 1930s when wages were approximately 30/- per week, the price of wheat was only 10/- per sack, so it was obvious that farming did not pay.

Like most parents we had various illnesses to contend with from time to time, which naturally resulted in extra work and expenses. The first serious trouble came in the Winter of 1934-5, when our elder daughter contracted whooping-cough in November, and very soon, as might be expected, the younger girl caught the complaint, and they were both very badly affected. As the younger one was only

3½ years old, there was a possibility that the choking might completely stop the breathing, especially during the night-time. The only way we knew of preventing this was to get her into a sitting position. There was no electric lighting in the house, so directly she began to cough I would slip out of bed, feel my way into the girl's bedroom, grab Dorothy and sit her up in bed. This happened sometimes two or three times each night for several weeks, and very often I was only half awake. In fact, sometimes in the morning I did not know if it was real or if I had been dreaming. In the meantime, our son, who was 8 months old became a victim of this distressing complaint, and as he was too young to be given effective medicine he developed Bronchitis and later Pneumonia and needed constant attention day and night. It was terribly hard for my wife who was six months pregnant at the time, and when the Doctor informed us that there was nothing more that could be done for the boy, she was very near to breaking point. Neither of us were prepared to accept that Jim was going to die, and we continued nursing him as best we could. In sheer desperation my wife made a hot drink from blackcurrant jam, and the pleasant smell and taste encouraged Jim to drink a cupful of it, and in a very few minutes it released the phlegm which he vomited up, and from then on his condition improved considerably. So much so, that the Doctor was amazed when he saw him the next day. This occurred towards the end of February, and one can imagine how thankful we were that in the following July Jim won second prize in the Best Baby competition at the Village Flower Show. By the time the children had all recovered, Spring weather had arrived and that meant plenty of work for the tractor, getting the land ready for the corn drill. Some of the fields were bordered by a ditch or cliff, and as I felt the warmth of the sun on me I had a very uncomfortable feeling that I might go to sleep and finish up in a ditch or the river with the tractor on top of me.

I had worked six days a week all through the winter, without one good night's sleep, and 'Oh Boy was I tired!'

Our fourth child, Millicent, was born in June 1935, and when she was eighteen months old we experienced our second serious family illness. As a result of visiting relatives who lived in another village, Millicent contracted a rather bad cold, the after effects of which was a discharge from both ears. The local doctor was called, and as there was no improvement within three days Millicent was sent to the Children's Ward at the Anglesea Road Wing of the Ipswich and East

Suffolk Hospital. Two days later Ruth was taken ill with a very high temperature, and the doctor quickly diagnosed Scarlatina, and immediately arranged for Ruth to be sent to the Fever Hospital at St Helen's, Ipswich. By this time Jim had developed Chicken-pox, which meant that Ruth had to be put into an isolation cubicle, and when in a few days, Jim had all the symptoms of the fever he was promptly given similar treatment. We still had Dorothy at home, and it seemed possible that she would escape both complaints, but on the tenth day she became ill, and it was soon obvious that she too was a victim of Scarlatina. So it was an ambulance ride for her, and as she had not had Chicken-pox, she also was put into a cubicle as a precaution. The position now was that we had the youngest girl at one hospital, where the rule that was in operation disallowed visitation until the end of six weeks, and the other three children were all in separate rooms at another hospital at the other side of Town. As I was working six days a week, the only opportunity that my wife and I had for visiting was on a Sunday afternoon, and after cycling eight miles, all we could do was to stand outside the hospital ward and talk to the three children in turn through the window. As it was the month of February that was not a very pleasant exercise. When we were allowed to visit Millicent, we received a shock. She was in a very nervous and frightened state, and was tied to the bedstead. She did not respond in any way to anything we said or did. We learned from a girl of thirteen years of age, who was a patient on the same ward, that Millie had been smacked very severely by a nurse on the first night she spent in the hospital, and consequently was frightened of anyone in uniform. Evidently neither the ward sister nor the doctor were aware of this incident, and concluded that they had a spoilt and difficult child on their hands, and thus to a great extent lost interest in her. In our anxiety we consulted our local doctor, and he agreed that it might be better for Millie if she were at home. So I wrote to the doctor at the hospital and very tactfully put this suggestion to him. Unfortunately, this gentleman did not take kindly to this idea, and informed us that we could "fetch the child as soon as we wished", which we did the same day. Although Millie had been in hospital for seven weeks, the discharge from her ears had not stopped, and the cause had not been discovered. Also, her mental condition had worsened, and it was several days before she spoke or smiled. Our family doctor arranged for the District Nurse to attend to Millie's ears, which were gradually drying up, but after a few days my wife became ill with a high temperature and sore throat and it was soon apparent that she also was a victim of Scarlatina. The doctor inadvertently prescribed a double dose of the new drug known and M and B, and in 24 hours the temperature had dropped and the soreness had gone from the throat. Unfortunately, the injection had been transferred to the kidneys, resulting in acute mephitis. So now we were in real trouble. My wife was ordered to bed, the district nurse was not allowed in the house, and neighbours were afraid to help because of the risk of spreading the fever. The other three children by this time had been discharged fom hospital, and two of them had returned to school. However, Millie's ears were getting worse through lack of attention.

In those days farm workers were not given annual holidays, and the terms of employment were simply "no work — no money", so the situation was very serious. The farm manager kindly agreed for me to "work by the hour", which meant that I could go and come as I chose, and although this resulted in a reduction in my weekly wage it did allow me time to prepare meals etc.

A further difficulty arose when our family doctor requested that Millie be taken to the hospital for a check-up, and it was quite obvious that I was the one who must take her. It was a very busy time of the year on the farm, and in addition to my losing four hours pay, the tractor would be idle when it was most important that it should be at work. There was no alternative, so very reluctantly I prepared to take Millie to the hospital. As I left the house my wife said to me that I must not leave Millie there. I will not go into details of the conversation that took place in the doctor's consulting room. Suffice it to say that it was a very unhappy ten minutes for me, at the end of which I was told very bluntly that "I could let Millie go into hospital again or else". What could I do? I was at the mercy of that doctor, so I consented and had the sad task of breaking the news to my wife. As a result of what I was told at the hospital, I came to the conclusion that the two doctors had been conferring with each other about Millie and her complaint, and were not prepared to accept what I believed to be fact, that the discharge from Millie's ears carried the Scarlatina germs.

As might be expected, I was becoming very tired and frustrated, and when the local doctor visited our house on the following Sunday I expressed my feelings in very plain language. I made it quite clear that if Millie was discharged from hospital in a similar condition as before I would put in a complaint to the Health Authorities. In less than three hours I had a visit from his senior partner, who did his best to smooth things out, but I was determined not to be silenced, and in the end he promised to have a talk with the hospital doctor, giving him all the facts. He evidently kept his word, because two days later we had a message telling us that Millie could come home, and when I went to fetch her I was very pleased with her condition. From then on Millie's health improved, as did my wife's although she always had kidney trouble, and when she died six years ago Renal Failure was given as the major cause of her death.

All this was the direct result of a visit to relatives who lived in a village where there a few cases of Scarlatina, although there were none in this particular family. Apart from one lad who was a passenger the next day in the car in which Millie was first taken to hospital, no other cases were reported, but it could have developed into an epidemic. One question that I have never found the answer to is, "Why did I escape?" Another question I ask myself is "How did I manage to keep going?" — and the answer to that surely is "By God-given strengths".

By the time our family had settled down to a normal pattern of life, fears were being expressed by many people that there was a strong possibility that another World War was near. There were soon signs that the British Government, together with authorities in Belgium, France, and Holland, were taking the threats of Hitler very seriously, and soon the whole country was thinking and talking in terms of defence.

I had been a member of the local Special Police Force for about ten years, and had been given very few duties to perform, but now we were being called together for lectures and exercises. I was asked to join the newly-formed Air Raid Service, while retaining the status of Special Constable, and as I had some First Aid training and experience, I willingly responded to this request. As time progressed the lectures etc. became more frequent, taking up a lot of time for all those who were involved, and men became less enthusiastic. The climax came in the summer of 1939. The village constable planned a special exercise to be carried out in darkness, and as it was explained to the group of Special Constables and Air Raid Wardens, everyone seemed willing to co-operate, until the Chief Air Raid Warden demanded that the operation should be carried on from 'dusk till dawn'. Suddenly the whole atmosphere of the meeting changed. It was harvest-time, and some of us were working from 6.30 a.m. till 8 p.m., and certainly were not prepared to give up the whole of a night's sleep. Objections were soon raised to this demand, a very heated argument followed, and resignations were threatened. One thing that added to the dissatisfaction was the fact that the man who made this very unreasonable demand was a 'Retired Gentleman', and therefore would be able to have a good rest during the next day. The following morning the Constable had a straight talk with the retired gentleman, with the result that the exercise was timed to begin at 9 p.m. and finish at 2.30 a.m., to which everyone agreed. As a matter of fact, I myself did not undertake the full 'stint'. The Constable came to me at about 1.30 a.m. and said, "I understand your wife is not very well, so you can slip off now." I gratefully accepted this opportunity to get a few hours' sleep.

Although farmworkers' wages had risen by about 15% since 1924, and three days annual holiday had been granted by the Agricultural Wages Board, living conditions were still far from satisfactory, and the pensioners were the hardest hit. In 1938 and the beginning of 1939 there was strong agitation for the Old Age Pension to be increased from ten shillings to twelve shillings and sixpence per week, but when this was brought before Parliament the government of the day agreed that the old people needed the extra money but claimed that the country could not afford it. When War was declared a few months later, millions of pounds were quickly found for armaments etc., and the cry went up, "No money for food, but plenty for guns."

In spite of the adoption of the 'Policy of Appeasement' by the Allied Governments, and the visit of Mr. Neville Chamberlain to Munich to sign an agreement with Hitler, preparations for War were made by both sides. A plan to evacuate as many people as possible from the most vulnerable places was put into operation and Holbrook was scheduled to receive children from Dagenham in East London. A local committee allocated the children to the various homes in the village and we were put down to receive three girls of school age. In the meantime, a cousin of mine, Reg Chatham, who lived in Romford, and who was suffering from a nervous breakdown, decided to bring his wife and family of two boys and a girl to our house for the duration. I paid a visit to the Committee, and explained the situation, requesting that they should find other accommodation for the Dagenham girls, and eventually homes were found for two of them. That left us with four adults, five girls and thee boys in a three-bedroomed house, and one can imagine the problems that followed.

We were just beginning to get ourselves sorted out when War was actually declared on the 9th September, 1939, a Sunday. Our family attended the village Methodist Chapel, and the congregation met for a short service and then dispersed to prepare as far as possible for the worst. I was, and still am, a Local Preacher in the Ipswich Circuit, and was appointed to preach at Bucklesham in the afternoon and evening. This entailed cycling twelve miles each way, and the return journey would have to be made after 'lighting up'. So, with the consent of the friends there, I decided to miss the evening service and return home in the daylight.

My duties in connection with Civil Defence, included manning with five other men a post near the Marsh Gate, Lower Holbrook. A rota had been drawn up, and a neighbour and I were to be on duty from 9.30 p.m. to 11.30 p.m. the same night. During this period we did some work in the trench that was being dug to be used as our headquarters. This, in fact, was never completed, as we all realized that it would be absolutely useless as a protection in the event of an air raid. When I returned home all the family had found a resting place, and were sound asleep, so I very quietly slipped into bed beside my wife after putting my cycle lamp on the floor close to the bed ready for any emergency. I had had a very busy day, and was just about worn out, so I quickly fell into a deep sleep, from which I was suddenly aroused by the 'wail of the siren'. I was out of bed like a shot and managed to kick the lamp under the bed which had been pushed up close to the wall to make room for a second bed to be put up. As we had no electric lighting in the house I had to crawl under the bed in my nightshirt to rescue the only means of light available. We had received instructions that if the siren went every man must report to his particular duty post at once. Accordingly, I smartly mounted my bicycle and left our enlarged family to look after themselves. When I reached the trench I found my namesake, George, in fits of laughter, which I thought was quite inappropriate. It was some minutes before he was able to control himself sufficiently to be able to tell us what it was all about. The gas masks and steel helmets for the six of us who were to man this post had arrived on the Sunday afternoon. So the head warden, who lived opposite the Marsh Gate, took them to his house. When he was awakened by the siren he jumped out of bed, only half awake, grabbed this bundle of equipment, and made a rush for the duty post. Firstly, he got wedged in the doorway, then two of the masks fell to the ground. His wife switched on the electric light, which caused Dick to curse and swear, and then in retrieving the masks he let three steel helmets fall. At this stage, George walked across the road to lend a hand, and was met by the helmets rolling down the pathway, which he thought was a great joke, and this brought more bad language from Dick. It took George several minutes to give all these details to the rest of the squad when they arrived, and when Dick had calmed down he joined in the fun also. So War or no War, we had quite a jolly time whilst waiting for the 'All Clear'. Meanwhile, up at my house, pandemonium reigned. The children woke up frightened, and could not understand what was happening. Some of them in strange beds did not even know where they were. Everyone was trying to find their clothes and get dressed by candlelight, and my wife was in a panic because she could not find her bra. To add to the confusion, one of the neighbours, whose husband was also on duty, became very frightened and came into our house bringing her young child with her. That was how World War Two began at No. 2 Wall Farm Cottages, Holbrook. At tea time the same day, Reg looked across the table to me and said, "If the siren goes tonight Warrie, I'm putting your uniform on and going on duty, and you can stay here with this lot. One such night in a lifetime is enough for me!"

CONCLUSION

In putting into writing these memories of the beginning of the Century, I have re-lived many of the experiences mentioned and have become more and more thankful that present living conditions, especially for the elderly and sick, are so much better than they were before the Second World War.

On reflection, I am puzzled as to why so many people are unhappy to-day. At the time of writing, the news has just been announced that the number of unemployed has passed the three million mark, and many people are attempting to compare the present situation with that which existed in the 1920s and 1930s. In my opinion, there is a very great difference, because although the actual number of unemployed is approximately the same, the percentage of the whole working force is much lower. Also, the financial help given to those affected is much greater than during the period of the previous Depression. Unfortunately, there are signs that both nationally and internationally, the Trade Recession is getting worse, and I believe that many people will have to accept a lower standard of living, but I earnestly pray that living conditions will never again be as bad as they were in the period between the two World Wars.